S0-BTS-044

About the Author

Pat Weymes is a recognised authority on selling and one of the outstanding sales trainers of his generation, having worked with such prestigious companies as Xerox and ITT. He is the author of several books on selling, sales training and sales management, including *A Handbook of Sales Training and Development* (Kogan Page). Pat's consultancy, WinWin Selling, offers web-based sales training for both managers and salespeople. His sales training course is currently being rolled out globally in IBM. Visit the WinWin Selling website at www.winwinselling.com or contact Pat directly at weymes@iol.ie.

WIN-WIN SALES MANAGEMENT

WIN-WIN SALES MANAGEMENT

A Powerful New Approach for Increasing Sales from Your Team

Pat Weymes

Oak Tree Press

Dublin

Oak Tree Press
Merrion Building
Lower Merrion Street
Dublin 2, Ireland
http://www.oaktreepress.com

A catalogue record of this book is
available from the British Library.

Hardback ISBN 1 86076 165 8
Paperback ISBN 1 86076 181 X

Printed by MPG Books, Bodmin, Cornwall.

Contents

For Cameron with love

Foreword

I first met Pat Weymes ten years ago. I had read his *Handbook of Sales Training and Development* and sought him out through the publisher. It was the only book I had come across written specifically for sales trainers and it was full of excellent and practical advice.

I found Pat to be a mine of information, full of enthusiasm and always willing to share his experiences and approaches with fellow sales trainers. I have recommended and used his books in much of my own client work. His book, *How to Perfect your Selling Skills*, has the distinction of being the one which clients and their salespeople consistently fail to return to me. I suspect that my continuing purchases have paid for several of his holidays.

Now Pat has allowed me to write this Foreword to his latest book, *Win-Win Sales Management*, written specifically for sales managers. He has long bemoaned the fact that there is so little advice available to those who train and manage the sales force when there is so much available for the sales people themselves. His book will be welcomed for that.

Like Pat, however, I have experienced the trauma of being promoted to run a sales force based solely on the fact that I was a successful and experienced salesman within the organisation. Pat's book will certainly be welcomed by those who find themselves in a similar position. However, experienced sales managers will also benefit from reading it, for he has again provided a lot of practical advice spiced with his own reflections and experiences. I too remember how little direct support salespeople may get from their managers and how misunderstood their role may be within their own organisations. Pat has shown in this book how wide the sales manager's brief might be and how great their influence might extend.

As with many complex disciplines, there is so much other good advice from Pat that could not be accommodated in this text — I foresee another book already on the horizon. A particular interest which we both share, for example, is the development of Internet selling and training, which he discusses and which is predicted to be perhaps the dominant form of selling in the future.

His customer-friendly, "non-technique" or win-win sales approach has found much favour with those who are fortunate to hear of it — not least with all of those involved in service or consultative selling.

Sales managers can so often be driven by monthly targets that they may forget to respect both their people and their principles. Read Pat's book and use it as a guide to further reflection of your own environment, behaviours and expectations. I admit that I found myself a little shamed with some of my own failings in the sales manager's role. If you do the same, I can only see benefits both for yourself and for those you manage and support. Whatever happens, let Pat know what you think about his book and how you have used it. I know that he will welcome your feedback.

Dr Michel Kearsley
Managing Director
Word*Com* Associates, UK

Acknowledgements

Indirectly, many great salespeople and sales managers have written this book, as it is their views and experiences that significantly influenced most of what you will read. The list includes salespeople from right across the spectrum of industry who I have had the privilege to work with or manage. I have encountered many sales managers, some great and some not so great, but all of them have made some contribution to my efforts; their views are used extensively throughout the pages of this book.

The biggest group by far was the 20,000 or so sales course delegates who I have worked with or met throughout my career in sales training and, ultimately, they are the only real experts on how they should be managed and motivated.

I wish to thank Frank Cairns who has helped me enormously with no fewer that seven different publications and has always been a great supporter — coming in with encouragement just when I needed it most. My UK associate Dr Mike Kearsley offered much valuable guidance at all stages of the book and was so supportive and patient with the never-ending changes and alterations. Thank you Mike; your assistance was greatly appreciated.

Last but not least, I wish to pay tribute to the efforts of the team in Oak Tree Press and in particular to my editor Brian Langan for his outstanding patience and support and great editing.

Preface

When I was offered my first sales management role, I was extremely nervous about accepting it for two reasons. Firstly, I was concerned about whether I could do the job and the very idea of standing up in front of a group of potentially aggressive salespeople was very scary. Secondly, I was also aware that very little supportive material was available to people like myself who had no skills in the motivation and development of a sales team. Yes, I had experienced managers all around me and there were management courses available that the company would be happy to have me attend.

I took the job and never missed an opportunity to attend training courses or enlist the guidance of wiser and more experienced managers. In terms of personal effectiveness, I found their guidance invaluable. I learned how to manage my time, analyse complex reports, work out detailed budgets and for the first time I had a clear understanding of how the company made a profit. Being able to draw on the experience of high profile experienced managers was a great education.

However, as the company had few sales managers available, I had to look elsewhere for help and guidance on subjects such as sales team motivation. I talked to as many as I could and listened attentively as they outlined the secrets to success in sales management.

Over time, I began to feel less and less comfortable about the "guidance" I was receiving from practically all quarters. Nearly all of this guidance focused on asserting authority, motivation through fear and monitoring salespeople to ensure they carried out their job — a job which, all sales managers agreed, salespeople were grossly overpaid to do! I could never buy into this "guidance" or indeed the examples I was expected to imitate. The fact that these "skills" didn't actually work seems to have been irrelevant. They might have learned something to their advantage had they spoken to the *experts* in how salespeople should be motivated — the salespeople themselves.

This book is all about win-win sales management attitude — a powerful set of values that will not only build but also sustain the motivation of your team indefinitely. It is not only about motivating salespeople, it is also about motivating yourself as the sales manager and how you can apply these skills to make your life better for yourself and your family. The real benefit of this book is that you don't have to invest in new systems or study for long periods of time to dramatically improve the motivation of your team. It only requires you to buy into and practise the skills of win-win sales management.

This book concentrates on three fundamentals of successful sales management. Firstly, your customers and what you, your salespeople and your company need to do to bring them back again and again. You must ensure that the guidance you (and your company) give your salespeople on *how to sell* to your customers is accurate and based on precise customer feedback — not somebody's personal opinions. In the opening chapter, "Win-Win Selling", I have put forward extensive researched views on what buyers think of selling and how they wish to be sold. Don't be surprised if you can see immediately on completing this chapter where your sales team are losing massive sales — and customers. It is not only salespeople that lose sales — it might even be you!

Secondly, we need to talk about you and the crucial role you play in the performance of the team and the achievement of your sales targets. Everything you do in association with your salespeople is highly contagious, so it stands to reason that you cannot motivate others if you are not a highly motivated person yourself. While this book concentrates extensively on personal motivation, it also details how sales management attitude and behaviour can build or shatter sales team morale.

Thirdly, we will discuss in depth the critical area of salespeople's motivation. This book uncovers the skills that sales managers should practise if they wish to get maximum performance from the team. The ideas that I outline are not just my personal opinions; they are the views of many thousands of salespeople who would have been delighted to share their views with their sales managers — if only their sales managers had taken the time to ask!

This book embraces many other important subjects, such as contracts of employment, sales meetings, setting and achieving sales targets and a host of other essential topics all written with one objective in mind: to help sales managers be better at what they do.

I learned all these skills the hard way and now I take some pleasure in sharing them with you. I hope you find them useful.

Pat Weymes
May 2000

Chapter One

Win-Win Selling

One thing that has always fascinated me about the sales profession is the failure of managers to take an active role in monitoring the way their salespeople do business with customers. If, by taking a new and radical slant on these important issues, I can encourage you to look again at your entire selling approach, I will have achieved a very important objective and you may be on the way to substantially increasing your sales.

Win-win is all about helping customers to make up their own minds. The tired old techniques of manipulation and forced selling have no place in today's sophisticated marketplace. The principle of win-win selling is one of collaboration: creating a mutually beneficial relationship in which the customer's needs can, if possible, be matched with your company's products or services. This principle of mutuality can be extended to encompass the role of the sales manager. The manager and sales team form a collaborative relationship in which the salespeople can express their concerns and problems and share their successes with their colleagues and managers, and the managers can provide encouragement, advice and motivation as needed.

Before discussing these principles in depth, let's have a look at present-day attitudes to selling.

Selling Attitudes

I believe the day will come when salespeople, like other professions, will have to study for a degree or a qualification in customer-friendly selling. Until the profession agrees benchmarks, standards and a code of ethics, we will always be at the mercy of other people's opinions on how to succeed in selling. The fact that these opinions come from people who never actually sold anything appears to be irrelevant. Anybody going into selling today just might be advised thus:

> "The first thing you have got to do is sell yourself."
>
> "You never take no for an answer."
>
> "You only get one chance to sell!"

These are just a few of the damaging and misinformed statements about this profession. While there are always salespeople whose ideas on selling leave a lot to be desired, they only help to reinforce the cynics' view that in order to succeed in selling, you must possess:

- A hard neck (presumably to take abuse and insults);
- The capacity to develop and deliver a sales "pitch" (whatever that may be!);
- The ability to convince people to buy things they don't actually need.

I need to make an up-front statement here. I am very proud of my profession and I consider it a privilege to have worked with so many superb successful salespeople from all parts of the world. I am firmly of the opinion that selling today is so much more professional than it was a few short years ago. It is because of my intense interest in this profession that I feel obliged to challenge those purveyors of manipulative sales techniques who clearly know nothing about modern-day selling and even less about how people buy. By doing so, I hope I am providing a useful service to my fellow professionals.

By way of illustration, during the time that I was writing this book, I watched a TV documentary on selling. It outlined the trials and tribulations of hundreds of men and women selling a particular product. Anybody who cares about this profession would be extremely disappointed with the selling message it conveyed. The programme took viewers through the sales training, which included inspiring guidance like, "In selling, *you never give up asking for the order*." Buyers admire persistence but have a serious problem with persecution. The company sales trainer had another piece of wisdom to offer: "People will mirror whatever you do, so keep agreeing with the customers and they will have to agree with you." Really?

Watching programmes like this, it is not surprising that the perceptions of the selling profession are so poor. The producers could have made this film in any one of many highly professional sales operations and yet they chose an example that would only reinforce people's belief that selling is a dreadful job! Not surprisingly, many of the fine people who joined this company only lasted a short time and, based on their exit interviews, will not be looking for another job in selling. The company projected itself as a cross between a brainwashing organisation and a religious order and by their own admission: "If you don't make it you have to go!" (If at first you don't succeed, you're fired!)

The company itself may have a different view. Undoubtedly, they are a successful company and I am sure that they can point to people who have made good money from selling their products. As a professional salesperson, I would be concerned about a couple of issues: First of all: the people who didn't make it were trained in what they thought were proper selling skills and are lost forever to the profession. This company put hundreds of people through their course and only a small minority survived more than three months; many of them made no money at all. What are they going to tell the world about this company? What are they going to tell the world about selling?

Reflective Activity

- As a sales manager, what is your opinion of what you have read about the sales profession?
- What selling messages do you or your organisation give to your salespeople?
- Does your company have a corporate selling philosophy — a set of values endorsed by management and practised by all salespeople?
- How can you be sure that all your salespeople are selling the right way — and more to the point, what is the "right way"?
- What do your customers really think about your salespeople and their selling approach?
- What does the rest of your organisation think about you and your sales team?
- As the sales manager, where do you place the greater emphasis: on getting sales or getting customers?
- Do you have high dropouts and if you have, what is the reason?
- Do people leave because they are not good enough?
- Do people leave because your company is not good enough?
- Are you sacrificing long-term customer business for short-term gain?
- Are you happy with the volume of repeat business you get from your customers?

Whenever I put these questions to sales managers, they usually say something like: "We must be doing something right because we always achieve our sales targets and our customers are not complaining."

An acquaintance of mine, who is the International Business Manager for a highly successful business product, told me about two of her franchisees operating in Central London. These companies sell exactly the same products and their arrangement is exclusive — they do not sell any other products — so both companies are operating on a level playing pitch.

One of these companies employs 22 people, 10 of whom are salespeople. The other company employs 36 people, 18 of whom are salespeople. The smaller company had a turnover in excess of 12 per cent greater that its larger rival in 1998. Not surprisingly, some of my friend's senior colleagues wanted to understand how the smaller sales team could totally outsell their rivals, so they went to talk to both of them. The larger company had been in operation longer and very significantly had finished off its first year with mediocre results. This mediocre company performance had a knock-on effect in setting sales targets in succeeding years and while they were achieving their targets, their profit performance was not even close to the smaller company.

The smaller company carried no such baggage. They started with a bumper year; that achievement became the benchmark for targeting all new salespeople and they have maintained that growth ever since.

SALESPEOPLE'S PERCEPTION OF SELLING

Many salespeople and even sales managers don't think very highly of their profession. This is probably why some salespeople often camouflage their selling role by using titles like:

"Account Executive"

"Marketing Consultant"

"Area Manager"

It's OK to use professional-sounding titles provided it is not the intention to deceive the customer or (more disappointingly) because a salesperson doesn't want people to think he or she is *only a salesperson.* We should all take heart from international research, which indicates that salespeople are amongst the highest paid earners in the world.

THE CASE IN FAVOUR OF WIN-WIN SELLING

My experiences over many years have convinced me that:

- Sales techniques are the ultimate "turn-off".
- Selling skills are positive — sales techniques are negative!
- People resent being "sold to".
- We should be looking for customers — not sales.
- To increase sales we must **stop** selling — yes, that's what I said!

I will discuss each of these points in detail shortly.

Like many experienced salespeople, I too have been indoctrinated in the need to develop techniques in order to maintain a competitive edge. Even today, sales consultants all over the world make a good living convincing trainees of the importance of developing these essential skills. Where I differ from my fellow sales training professionals is my unshakeable belief: *sales techniques are outdated and no longer applicable.*

I have never felt comfortable with the suggestion that techniques or programmed responses are required to elicit a sale from a customer. This is not to imply that all sales training is only about techniques — it most certainly is not! In fact, many of the more positive skills I learned on my first sales course, I use to this very day.

Sales managers and trainees exaggerate the need to develop techniques when the evidence clearly states that their influence in the sale is minimal. In support of this statement, random buyers were asked to prioritise the following selling attributes in order of influence in the buying decision. Try it yourself and rate the following skills in order of importance as if you were the buyer:

- Communication skills
- Fluency of speech
- Integrity of the salesperson
- Personal appearance
- Ability to listen
- Sales technique
- Pleasing personality
- Interested in learning about your company
- Interested in telling you about his or her company
- Expertise in product knowledge.

My company delivers web-based sales training around the world and one of the assignments students complete, as part of their course, is to interview three friendly buyers and seek their opinions on what they consider to be most influential selling skills. The first 1,500 responses indicated clearly that buyers, no matter where they operated in the world, considered technique to be of no importance whatsoever. Now compare your ratings against those endorsed by buyers:

1. Integrity of the salesperson
2. Ability to listen
3. Interested in learning about your company
4. Expertise in product knowledge
5. Communication skills
6. Pleasing personality
7. Personal appearance
8. Fluency of speech
9. Interested in telling you about his or her company
10. Sales technique.

If you agree with other buyers, you will also conclude that typical sales training tends to place too much emphasis on techniques and would be better invested in the development of more positive, customer-friendly skills. Now let me take the points mentioned earlier one by one.

"Techniques" — the Ultimate "Turn-off"

Salespeople do not learn sales techniques out of cynical motivation; it has always been assumed that they are an integral part of the selling role.

What we have here is a major clash in perceptions. Some buyers perceive the blatant use of techniques as an insult to their intelligence. Some techniques are so jaded that customers can actually identify many of them, such as the "boomerang method", the "sharp angle close" and the "if" technique. Remarkably, nobody seems to have taken time out to see if "techniques" actually increase sales or to measure salespeople's performance on the basis of "before and after".

Reflective Activity

- How often do you research your customer views about your selling approaches?
- How much research do you undertake to define what your salespeople do and say?
- Are you sure that they copy what they are told in sales training?
- Are you sure that the messages they receive in training are good advice?
- Do you give mixed messages when you yourself work with your salespeople?
- How do you know that other approaches would not be more successful?
- What do your customers think about your competitors?

- How do your competitors sell? Is there an opportunity here?
- Chances are good that you don't know all the answers. Should you have this information and if you should, whose job is it to find out?

If buyers viewed techniques in a positive light, presumably we would never hear them say, "Let's skip the 'sales talk' — just tell me what it does."

Just to make an important point: I read a recently published book on selling. The chapters had titles such as "Techniques for handling objections" and "How to close more sales". Having read through these chapters, the author would be hard pressed to convince me these skills were not designed to manipulate.

Selling Skills are Positive — Sales Techniques are Negative

Buyers are extremely impressed with what they discern as skilful selling! In their view, professional selling is *"something that is happening up front and we can see the skills in action!"*

It could be a combination of admirable attributes in the salesperson such as:

- Enthusiasm for the job and his or her company;
- Skilful fact-finding and genuine interest in helping the customer solve a problem;
- The overall integrity of the presentation;
- Knowledge of the market, product and competitive activity;
- A personalised and professionally produced proposal.

People Resent Being "Sold to"

The timeworn selling philosophy of "keep asking for the order" sits very uncomfortably with the old axiom: "A man convinced against his will is of the same opinion still." Both of these statements cannot be right! I have great sympathy with fellow professionals who are constantly under pressure to sell — after all, that is what they were employed to do. However, I'm sure you have witnessed a sales manager saying to salespeople:

> "See a lot of customers and ask them all to buy"
>
> "Remember the ABC of selling — always be closing"
>
> "Persistence is the key to success — so keep asking for the order"

I believe that these are diametrically opposed to everything that professional selling is all about. If you are in a business where your orders or products can be repeated or upgraded, your salespeople will not enhance customer relations by persecuting the buyer for the order when common sense would suggest that *the customer is not ready to buy at this moment!*

One example of this poorly thought out pressure selling we can all identify with is the visit to the local department store to buy some new clothes. The moment you walk in, the following scenario begins:

A salesperson comes over to you and asks, "Can I help you?"

Most people will respond with, "No thank you, I am just looking around."

You start looking through a rack of clothes and you begin to feel the sales assistant's hot breath on the back of your neck, and he or she says, "Was there something in particular you were looking for?"

You reply, "No, nothing in particular," as you investigate the quality of a garment.

Again the salesperson asks, "Would you like to try it on?"

To be fair to the salespeople, they think they are helping the customer. However, suppose they were to change their approach to: "May I be of service to you right now or would you like to have a look around?"

This is not another "technique". Do you see the difference? In the first example, the salesperson is obviously trying to get the customer to buy. On the other hand, in the latter example, the customer has a choice and they are not expected to make that buying decision on the spot. Every day, millions of people all over the world are exposed to this level of pressure to buy and the majority of people protest with their feet and walk out! We all need to be reminded that we are not in the business of selling — we are in the business of helping people to buy.

Your salespeople may not sell clothes in a department store, but they may also have standard approaches. How many times have you been told that you have been specifically chosen from thousands for a special offer? How often have you been told, "this is not a sales call" when that is exactly what it is?

Let's Look for Customers — Not Sales

There is a major attitudinal difference in salespeople who go out looking for sales and those who go out looking for customers. I view this as one of the most serious weaknesses in our profession. Too many sellers are only interested in the bottom line — to get a sale. Their selling strategy is based on brief short-term relationships and once their business is concluded, they turn their attention to the next prospect. Putting it in brutal terms, the sales plan is to get in, get a sale and get out!

Sales managers who encourage their salespeople to look for sales are ignoring the fact that each customer presents the opportunity to develop a long-term relationship with potential for repeat and referral business. If a member of your sales team pressurises a customer into a one-off sale in order to hit your managerial monthly target, they (and you) are being short-sighted. The objective is to build a solid but expanding customer base in which your own satisfied network of customers are your best advocates in the marketplace. This is a medium to long-term strategy, which creates customer strengths for you and your company. This form of thinking relates to the oldest principle in history: seedtime and harvest. You will also have created a business on the basis of truly servicing the needs of your customers.

One of the worst aspects of short-termism is the belief that you must separate your market into prospects and suspects! The first are those who might buy now and the others those who won't buy now. Looking down your nose at your customer base is devoid of vision and can never lead to the thriving cash-flow business; in fact, this attitude could put you out of business.

Some managers can stumble on their way to success, but the sort of short-termism discussed here is a roadmap for failure. The result is poor selling hit rates (ratio of calls to sales).

The IBM Way

Of course, excellent companies like IBM have very clear policies on how they wish their salespeople to sell and nobody could accuse IBM of not being a successful company. In *The IBM Way*, Buck Rodgers says:

> The rep has to know the customer's business in order to understand his problems; he also has to know his own product line if he is going to be of any help to the customer. And he has to know what the competition has to offer. . . . The people in the field have to be a combination of analyst, consultant, applications specialist and salesperson — and they have to be good in every area.

More importantly, he also goes on to say:

> Too many companies think only of their reps as salespeople, their primary and perhaps only function being to persuade a prospect to buy their product. If the prospect doesn't need the product, the salesperson is expected to create an illusion of need — then get the money and run before the reality sets in. That's not IBM's approach.

Common sense would tell you that it should not be anybody's approach.

The Benefits of Looking for Customers

Salespeople who go out looking for customers have a completely different approach. They recognise that there are many steps to creating customers and their first call is just for the purpose of establishing rapport and fact-finding. Salespeople who look for customers:

- Recognise the importance of building relationships;
- Are more relaxed in the initial approach (they are not trying to "sell" on this call);
- Realise the importance of proper fact-finding;
- Get more valuable information — as there is less pressure;
- Create an impression because they do something different (others are trying to get a sale);
- Have plenty of time to consider a creative response (not under pressure to come up with solutions on the spot);
- Tend to have extremely high hit rates (less calls and more quality sales); instead of calling on 100 customers to get 10 sales, they may call on 50 customers twice but get 20 or more sales.

This two-call-close concept nearly always causes some dismay when I introduce it in sales training. As one group of salespeople explained:

> Our sales manager has always made it clear to us that if we don't get the business on the spot, we are leaving the order there for our rivals — there is no way he is going to buy into this concept.

They were absolutely right, he would have nothing to do with it. He was too late — the salespeople decided to give it a try and it was so successful the two-call-close concept is now standard sales policy.

Reflective Activity

- How are your salespeople trained and guided?
- What is their tone and attitude to customers?
- What is their attitude to their sales targets?
- What is their attitude to you and the organisation?

If You Want to Increase Sales — Stop Selling!

An excellent definition of win-win selling is "helping people to make up their minds" and the best way to achieve this is by:

- Uncovering precisely what buyers are trying to achieve;
- Being personally convinced that your product or service is a solution;
- Explaining precisely how your product addresses your customers' needs;
- Offering reassurance when they express their concerns;
- Providing supporting information to assist them in making the purchase.

Let's compare this with one of the cardinal mistakes that even experienced salespeople are inclined to make: they start "selling" the product or service without the most basic of fact-finding information. In many cases, buyer needs are only of secondary consideration, and in these circumstances, selling is extremely difficult!

It is grossly unfair to generalise, but in my experience these are among the most serious mistakes made by salespeople today:

- Using a poorly thought out selling method — starting the interview by telling the buyer all about the salesperson's wonderful company. At this stage of the selling process, this information is totally irrelevant; the salesperson should be fact-finding, *not* selling.

- Similar to the above but not quite the same: offering a solution *before* the salesperson has accurately uncovered the problem. To use a medical analogy, consider the implications of a doctor writing up a prescription without doing any investigation!
- Trying to *sell* on the first call. This is a serious problem for many salespeople and this approach has "no sale" written all over it. Many salespeople think that if they don't get the sale on the first call, the order will go to a competitor. When they subsequently discover that the order did in fact go to a rival, it serves to reinforce their belief that they should have "nailed" the customer the first time. The solution here is to see this prospective sale as a two-call close: the first call *only* to fact-find and the second call to offer the solution.
- Inability to control the fact-finding interviews. What actually happens is that the salesperson becomes the interviewee rather than the interviewer and unwittingly passes over total control to the buyer. In these circumstances, salespeople usually find themselves defending the product, answering objections and *selling* when all they *should* have been doing was getting information.

"Selling" is something that happens at the second meeting and *never at the first*. If you want to increase sales dramatically, remember, the *last* thing you do is sell.

Conclusion

Apart from my own views and experiences on the merits of practising non-manipulative selling, there are a few other persuasive sources:

- Contrary to entrenched sales training messages, I've found no properly researched evidence that techniques have any positive influence on today's buyer or the outcome of the sale.
- We do know that senior buyers are not impressed with the use of techniques and in some cases could actually encourage them not to buy!
- Given the choice, buyers would prefer that salespeople were "up front" in all their dealings.
- While sales techniques may score highly in the classroom, they are of least importance at the sales interview.

A win-win selling style will help to create a co-operative rather than a competitive selling environment simply because the salesperson is no longer looked on as a predator or an opponent. Once buyers are convinced that sales will not be made at their expense, that the salesperson is genuinely trying to solve the customer's problems, then the seller/buyer relationship is transformed.

Ten Key Points from the Concept of Win-Win Selling

1. Does your company have a corporate selling philosophy — a set of values endorsed by management and practiced by all salespeople?
2. How can you be sure all your salespeople are selling the right way — and more to the point, what is the right way?
3. How often do you research your customer views about your selling approaches?
4. Make the decision — are you in the business of getting sales or getting customers?
5. If mutual trust is the key to successful selling, where does that leave pushy sales techniques?

6. In the views of buyers, sales techniques have no influence in the buying decision and in fact, could actually be the cause of them not buying.
7. Help your salespeople to understand that if they wish to increase their sales — the last thing they need to do is sell!
8. People resent being "sold to".
9. Win-win selling encourages a co-operative rather than a competitive selling environment.
10. Above all else, integrity is the key to successful selling.

Chapter Two

Keeping Yourself Motivated

If there is one role where success is dependent on self-motivation, it has to be the role of the sales manager. You cannot reasonably expect your salespeople to be any more motivated about their job than you are about yours. As the leader of the team, salespeople will look to you to charge up the atmosphere, infect them with your enthusiasm and radiate confidence. As a team, they can achieve just about anything. But how does the sales manager build and sustain personal motivation? Let's look at the key attributes:

- Confidence
- Self-image
- Attitude
- Clear goals.

Not only are these attributes fundamental to the management of people, all four elements are so strongly interlinked that they are interdependent; take any one element away from the remaining three and you are left with none!

We will look at each of these attributes in a moment but first let us understand why they are so important to sales managers. Not only will you have to motivate the sales team, but during the working day you will also probably employ the skills of a:

- *Financial controller*: because you will be operating within budgetary guidelines and this may also involve tricky questions before the board.
- *Trainer*: coaching the sales team in the art of win-win selling.
- *Public speaker*: addressing the sales team, speaking at training seminars and occasionally responding to after-dinner invitations at industry-wide level.
- *Counsellor*: re-motivating the discouraged and comforting those devastated by failure.
- *Diplomat*: picking your way through awkward situations and letting people down gently.
- *Psychologist*: sorting out salespeople's confused priorities and replaying it back to them in a manner they understand.

Experienced sales managers would also add other skills to that list. Sometimes the ability to juggle with sales targets will occasionally come in handy. Trying to apply these very special skills is difficult without outstandingly high levels of confidence and motivation. It is next to impossible. So lets take a look at each attribute.

Maximising Self-confidence

Confidence comes from the belief in our ability to do certain things. The only way we can develop that belief is through activity, through doing more things. This inevitably means taking risks, facing fear and experiencing failure. The lessons learnt from failure help build confidence. A baby taking its first steps will wobble and fall many times but in its determination to walk will dismiss completely all the failed efforts. As Confucius said, failure is not falling down; it is falling down and refusing to get back up again.

Don't Listen to the Cynics

Confidence is a mixture of positive and negative traits but when our confidence is low we tend to dwell on the negatives only. Sales managers are not immune to negative influences and there will always be people around to test your patience and self-belief. It may be a key salesperson who doesn't believe sales targets can be achieved or someone whose opinion is important, failing to see the wisdom of your new ideas. However, it is important to put people's opinions into perspective: it is estimated that when looking for support for a new idea, a whopping 97 per cent of people will be able to tell you why *it will not* work. How many times have you had your enthusiasm for an idea or project dampened by someone saying any of the following?

> "Sounds much too good to be true."
>
> "Take my word for it, it's not as simple as it seems."
>
> "You may as well dream here as in bed."
>
> "If it was that easy, how come someone else hasn't done it before now?"
>
> "It s not what you know, its who you know."

Look at the following quotation. Is it an accurate reflection of our times?

> Our earth is degenerate. Bribery and corruption are common. Children no longer obey their parents. The end of the world is evidently approaching.

This quotation could have come from this morning's newspaper but not so; it was carved on a stone slab in Assyria in 2800 BC.

In more recent times, the head of the US patents office wanted to close it down because he believed that everything worthwhile had already been invented — he made that remarkable claim in 1860. I approached senior people in a bank seeking finance for a major Internet project — they turned it down on the basis that the Internet was too new and too much of a gamble — this was in 1996. So much for the creative talents of people whose job it is to invest in futures.

Learn from Experience

A common denominator of successful sales managers is that they are excellent students of their profession. They are the epitome of what Lord Chesterfield said:

> There are three classes of people in this world. The first learn from their own experience — these are the wise. The second learn from the experience of others — these are the happy. The third neither learn from their own or the experiences of others — these are the fools.

In an early sales management role, I worked with people who weren't overly excited about taking on any role that involved confrontation or a high risk of failure. Subsequently, I have met many others who suffer from the same "fear-of-failure" mentality. Common sense will tell you that if you are so entrenched in avoiding failure, it is inevitable that you will also avoid success — it is the worst possible mentality for a sales manager.

In one of my sales management roles, whenever some serious management/staff situation had to be confronted, key people went "missing" and I was left to deal with the situation. Through my inexperience, I made many serious mistakes but learned to correct them whenever a similar situation recurred. The more experience I got the more serious tasks I took on. This culminated in developing management skills that no ordinary sales management role would ever provide. I didn't design it that way, but I am grateful that it happened nonetheless and the experience of handling such difficult situations has helped me enormously in my career.

Dealing with difficult situations inevitably meant making difficult choices and I used a formula that I use to this very day. When you are also faced with adversity you might want to try it out. Ask yourself; what is it about this situation that bothers me?

What can I do about it? List your choices. What is the worst that can happen if I take action and what are the implications if I don't? Outlining your choices on a piece of paper doesn't make your problems go away but it certainly helps to put them into perspective. Remember, you will always have a choice. You can:

- Fight it!
- Flee it!
- Forget it!
- Face it!

List on a piece of paper the top three circumstances that negatively impact your motivation. It might be your current relationship with your bank, conflict at work, at home or a concern about your health. Try out the above formula and if it works for you, continue to use it in future.

Make the Big Decision

At some stage in your career you need to make a decision: do you want to be mediocre or do you want to be the very best at what you do? It will always be easy to be mediocre but if you are going to be the best it is really going to hurt. As in all professions, sales managers generally fall into one of three categories: poor, mediocre and outstanding.

- 10 per cent are very poor at what they do;
- 80 per cent are in the mediocre to good category;
- 10 per cent are outstanding — because they give that extra effort.

Duncan Goodhew, the British Olympic gold medallist, put the importance of "giving that little extra" into context when he said: "I spent a great deal of my young life in a swimming pool, constantly trying to improve my speed. I eventually won a gold medal by one-thousandth of a second — in other words, a little extra." Martina Navratilova was once asked what special qualities she possessed that made her such an outstanding talent. She replied: "When I turned professional I had to make a decision. I always knew it would be easy to be mediocre, but if I was going to be the best, it was really going to hurt! The rest is history."

Make the decision right now to do whatever is necessary to be in this top 10 per cent. While all the suggested steps may look daunting, a journey of a thousand miles starts with the very first step.

Brush up Your Self-image

Our imagination plays a bigger part in our lives than most of us realise and will power is not the dominating factor in achieving our goals. When our imagination is in conflict with our will, imagination wins every time. For example, if you will yourself to be successful at something while at the same time imagining that you will fail, it is impossible to succeed. If, on the other hand, you can imagine yourself succeeding, you're half way there. However, will power and imagination working in tandem are an unbeatable force.

The power of imagination has been well documented in cases of hypnotism and autosuggestion. Many of us are "hypnotised" into thinking we are destined to be failures, so we behave appropriately. If you see yourself as a shy, unassertive, mediocre sales manager, your behaviour will tend to support your own concept of who you are. Go into any negotiating situation thinking you will lose and in practically every case you will find that you were right.

Emile Coue, the nineteenth-century French physicist, was famous for his amazing cures through the method of autosuggestion. Remember the phrase *every day in every way I am getting better and better*? He believed that the imagination was the key to self-cure. There is plenty of hard factual evidence to support his suggestions. Hospital beds all over the world are filled with people whose only reason for being there is that they imagine they are seriously ill. People have died when they should have lived, while others have lived when they should have died, all through either negative or positive imagination.

Dr Maxwell Maltz has spent many years researching the subconscious power. His book *Psycho-Cybernetics* is hailed as a classic in its field and tells us that:

> The nervous system cannot tell the difference between an imagined and a real experience and the nervous system reacts appropriately to what we imagine to be true.

For example, if you ate spaghetti but subsequently thought you had eaten worms — you would probably become quite ill!

If you think negatively, the result will be negative, whereas if you think positively you will create an atmosphere that makes positive results almost a certainty.

A couple of questions for you to ponder: If you didn't know how old you were, what age would you feel you were? How would you feel on Monday morning if you thought it was Saturday morning?

Practise What You Can't Do!

As indicated, good sales managers need to develop a multitude of talents; it is the exceptional person who comes into the profession with all the skills. Once you have identified a weakness that is holding you back, start working on it now! Don't say:

> "I am not cut out to be a sales manager"
>
> "I am fearful of making presentations to large groups"
>
> "Senior salespeople intimidate me"
>
> "I am a poor letter writer"
>
> "I am not an assertive person"

Start saying "that's the way I used to be but today is a different story". To offer some personal reassurance: throughout my life I have always had an innate fear of speaking in public; today I make my living from it!

Avoid Negative Comparisons

Avoid measuring your success by what you have done compared with others, but compared with what *you are capable of doing*. I have seen what this negative comparison can do to the longer-term development of a salesperson. At an annual performance review, a conversation went like this between a salesperson and her manager.

> *Manager*: "While you have done quite well, I really do need you to improve your sales figures this year. Compared with Sharon, your figures are not great."
>
> *Salesperson*: "But you wouldn't expect me to be as good as Sharon — after all she is the top salesperson?"
>
> *Manager*: "No, I wouldn't expect you to be as good as Sharon, but I expect you to try."

Here is a woman who didn't think very highly of herself or her selling skills, and her sales manager now *confirmed* her selling deficiency. Perhaps if the salesperson had kept Eleanor Roosevelt's comments in mind: "nobody can make you feel inferior without your consent", she might have reacted differently. Sadly, that young woman never achieved a sales target in her remaining five years with that company. The role of the salesperson and the sales manager is difficult enough without listening to soul-destroying comments.

To ensure that you maintain a confident self-image:

- Shy away from negative people — they will never pay your mortgage;
- Work on the attitudes of salespeople and those around you who eat into the morale and motivation of yourself and your team;

- When you have a negative thought, dilute it with plenty of positives;
- Develop yourself and your skills to the point where you will always have career choices — staying in a job because you have to will do little for your self-esteem, confidence or motivation;
- Develop an unshakeable "yes I can" mentality.

It has been said that a man flattened by an opponent will get up again but a man flattened by conformity stays down for good. Remember that it is not *what you think you are* that holds you back, its *what you think you are not!* And finally, here is an amusing reminder, which I believe to be from Mark Twain: "I have suffered a great many catastrophes in my life — none of which actually happened."

Develop Better Attitudes

If you have a negative attitude towards life, chances are you will also project a negative personality and it is what others see that matters — particularly where relationships are concerned. The opposite is also true. There is really little difference between people. The little difference is attitude, but the big difference is whether the attitude is positive or negative. If you tend to have a lot of conflict in your dealings with others, it's time to look at your attitude to ensure that you are only part of the problem, not THE problem.

There is hardly a sales manager in the world that hasn't been brainwashed on the need to project a positive mental attitude, but it is important to remember that positive thinking can help you in more ways than one.

Most of us in selling know that a positive outlook is a powerful force for personal and professional success. However, various reports also demonstrate that an upbeat attitude can increase sales, cure a headache, ward off the 'flu, improve a tennis game, reduce depression and help us to live longer!

Dr Christopher Petersen of the University of Michigan has conducted studies which lead him to claim that optimism can help to fight off illness and dramatically improve the social side of our lives!

In one of his studies, he used questionnaires to divide test subjects into two groups. People who had control over their lives were labelled optimists. Those who expected the worst and saw themselves as victims were identified as pessimists! He found that over the course of a year a confirmed pessimist is twice as likely to experience minor illness, such as the 'flu or a sore throat, than the optimist. After further investigation, he concluded that a long-term pessimistic attitude can lead to more disabling diseases and a host of other medical problems!

In another study, Dr Martin Seligman of the University of Pennsylvania interviewed and tracked the health of 99 World War II veterans over a period of 35 years. Pessimistic respondents were more likely to have health problems such as hypertension, diabetes or back trouble and were more likely to die many years earlier than those whose outlook was clearly optimistic! By taking a more optimistic view of living, you can also improve relationships at work, at home and in your social life. Positive people with positive attitudes infect others by their very presence, whereas "whiners" rarely get their audience to return for a second performance! One comedian summed it up when he said: "When you tell people your troubles, 95 per cent of people don't care and the other 5 per cent are glad!"

A humorous story is told about two men named Sam and Jed who determined that they would become wealthy by hunting wolves. In their part of the country, a $7,000 bounty was offered for each wolf captured alive. Day and night, the two partners searched mountains and forests seeking the valuable prey. Exhausted one night, they fell asleep dreaming of their potential fortune. Suddenly Sam awoke to see that they were surrounded by about 50 wolves with flaming eyes and bared teeth. Sam gently nudged his friend and said: "Jed, wake up! We're rich!"

Develop Unshakeable Inner Belief

It is remarkable what people with unshakeable belief can achieve. Walt Disney was said to have asked ten people for their views on a new project and when all ten were unanimous in their *rejection* of it, he would begin to work on it immediately.

Similarly, if everybody thinks you have come up with a great idea, you may be well advised to think again. Henry Ford is reported to have held up plans for a new automobile because every single member of his management was in favour. He is reported to have said, "Let's think again, I don't like unanimous decisions." Subsequently, the project was ditched and the company saved millions of dollars.

People with progressive ideas put up with a certain amount of ridicule from the cynics of this world, but take consolation in the knowledge that no monument was ever erected in memory of a critic.

To sustain positive reinforcement, carry out this positive activity frequently. Take a few minutes to write down all the positive qualities you possess. For example:

- *I dress well and I look professional.*
- *Salespeople react well to my guidance.*
- *I am good at interpersonal relationships.*
- *I have made a happy family life.*
- *I have many uniquely positive management skills.*
- *I consider myself a top sales manager.*
- *I am open-minded and prepared to learn.*
- *I am a free-thinking individual with career choices.*

Write up a diary of all of your personal achievements and add to them regularly. Whenever you are feeling a little low or your confidence has taken a dive, take out the list and review the contents — it will give you the lift you need.

Turning Defeat into a Positive Learning Experience

We have all experienced defeat. It may have been a major sale, a broken romance, a lost job, a failed exam or losing a top salesperson. The reason for the defeat is not the problem; how we choose to react is what's crucial. According to Paul J. Meyer, president of Success Motivation Institute, "Ninety per cent of all those who fail in life are not actually defeated; they simply quit."

Defeat is not synonymous with failure unless we allow it to be. Defeat is an unavoidable part of life. But if we can rise above self-pity, think positively, learn from experience, examine alternatives, maintain a sense of humour and set new goals, we can turn a bad experience into a good one!

Don't Become Your Own Worst Enemy

Did it ever cross your mind when looking in the mirror that you may be looking at your number one competitor? Your daily behaviour and general attitude could cost you dearly.

Reflective Activity

Try to answer these questions honestly:

- Do you always listen to the news before you start work?
- Are you usually in good humour in the mornings?
- Do you always speak well of others?
- Are you good-natured about a decision that goes against you?
- Do you try to see the positive points in people?
- Are you easily offended?
- Are you always punctual?

Let's be honest about this, listening to the news may put you in an alert and interested frame of mind but it may also dampen your good humour — essential to maintaining a positive working environment. There is also the added danger that you will use this "bad news" as a way to break the ice with contacts. It may get them talking, but will it do anything for their motivation?

It is quite human to make hasty judgments about others but it would certainly help to build better relationships if we can train ourselves to look for *positives*.

One other crucial aspect of this activity is punctuality, which many see as "arriving on time", but it is a lot more. It is delivering on your promises within the timeframe you originally claimed and dealing with your salespeople's urgent requests — *today*!

See Problems as Opportunities

One of the pillars of professional sales management is the ability to remain optimistic even when faced with what appears to be total ruin.

Dale Carnegie, author *of How To Win Friends and Influence People*, used to tell a story of a New England man who inherited a farm in Florida. On his arrival, he discovered the farm was made up of sandy soil on which no crops would grow, and if that wasn't enough, the place was also infested with rattlesnakes. Undeterred, he decided to become a rattlesnake farmer. He sold the skins for women's handbags and shoes and sold snake venom to hospitals for use as a serum. So many people heard of his achievements and wanted to visit that the town thrived as a tourist attraction.

The ultimate tribute came when the local townspeople decided to rename their town: Rattlesnake, Florida.

The farmer was not put off by the circumstances or by what he saw. What he identified in his mind was an opportunity to utilise what others thought was unusable. Common sense and imagination became allies in a new adventure.

Avoid Confusing Fact with Opinion

In my years of working with sales managers, I never cease to be amazed at the way so many really good people confuse facts with opinions. In practically every case, it is the opinion that is most damaging. Frequently I hear:

> "That company is obviously in trouble, because they have made several people redundant."
>
> "My month is ruined because I have lost two of my top salespeople."

In the first case, it may be a fact that people have been made redundant but it is only an *opinion* that the company is in trouble. In the second case, it is a fact that you have lost two of your top salespeople but it is only an *opinion* that your month is ruined. Sales managers are also the victims of their own negative opinions. I hear managers say, "He is making the calls but he is not getting the sales and therefore his problem is his *inability to close the sale*." This is a dangerous assumption to make because the salesperson may be sent on a course to correct his closing methods when his problem may be his *inability to open the sale*.

Reflective Activity

Dale Carnegie once said that the way to acquire enthusiasm is to believe in yourself and what you are doing, if you want to get something definite accomplished. But how enthusiastic are you? Take a few moments to reflect on these questions. How much do you truly believe:

- In yourself and your ability to do the job?
- In the integrity of your salespeople and your company?
- In your product or service?
- In your profession and the industry that you represent?

And are you:

- Open to the views of other people?
- Discouraged by failure or negative comments from others?
- Prepared to make mistakes in an effort to learn?
- Prepared to persevere in the face of opposition or ridicule?
- Anxious to consider every possible angle?
- A believer that to every problem there is a solution?

The sales manager who truly believes in each of these areas will automatically feel enthusiastic and in so doing will automatically enthuse the salespeople.

CLEAR GOALS

Unless you have clear goals on where you want to be in two or five years from now, and an action plan to achieve these goals, it is almost impossible to be motivated. Motivation literally means "inspiration to action". There are two types of motivation. External motivation operates through fear or incentive imposed by external influences such as, for example, you as the sales manager. This type of motivation is short-term and ceases once the need or fear has been satisfied or eliminated.

The second type of motivation, internal motivation, is the more powerful, because it is long-term and alters inbred attitudes. It comes from developing a sincere desire for the things that you want most out of your job, your career and your life. Before we discuss the importance of goals, let's do a little soul-searching; please answer these questions as honestly as you can:

- What major achievements have you had in the past year?

- What promises did you make to yourself that you failed to act on?
- What promotions have you had in the past two years?
- What real improvements have you made in your living standards?
- What are you doing today that you were also doing two years ago?
- What do you expect to be doing in five years?
- Have you written goals for what you really want out of life?
- Are you presently realising your full potential?

Your answers to these questions are important; if you have answered predominantly in the negative it should be clear to you that you have a lot of work to do in setting and achieving career goals. To aid your long and short-term motivation it is vital to retain a sense of direction. Be crystal-clear about what you want and keep the benefits of your goals at the front of your mind all the time.

The Importance of Setting Goals

Strange as it may seem, many people plan their holidays better than they plan their lives. Anytime I meet de-motivated people, I only have to ask them where they expect to be in 12 months' time and the shrug of the shoulders tells me all I need to know. Real motivation comes from setting and achieving personal and business goals — so be crystal-clear about what it is you want. If your motivation requires a major boost, there is every chance that the solution lies in taking the time out to write up your goals. Clear unambiguous goals will help you to:

- Build purpose into everything you do — at work and in your personal life;
- Differentiate between achievement and activity — fundamental to building and maintaining self-confidence;

- Provide that special magic that helps sustain long-term motivation;
- Transform being into living.

Life is often compared to a weighing scale: invest too much time in one area at the expense of the others and you will upset the balance.

Personal Goals are Imperative

It is part of our nature as human beings to strive towards some desirable goal. If we have nothing to aim for, we become bored and frustrated. The solution is to take charge of your life. Replace the frustration with some action planning and spend your time and energy agreeing your goals in an effort to making your life better for yourself and your family.

Imagine a couple who have decided to spend their lives together. However, one wants to live in the country and the other in the city. As they are trying to achieve two separate goals, the harmony of the relationship is obviously at risk. Imagine the opposite: both working as a team trying to achieve the same common objective — this is an unbeatable force and continuous motivation is assured!

The importance of adding your personal goals is reflected in this piece of wisdom: in the history of mankind, there has never been a case of anybody on his deathbed saying "I wish I had spent one more day in the office."

Think BIG

I recall one salesperson that consistently returned a performance (and earnings) three times greater than the average. He wasn't better looking, better dressed, more experienced or any more skillful than the others — the only difference was that he thought three times bigger.

The other salespeople had made the mistake of looking on our corporate quota as the ceiling when they should have been looking on it as the minimum.

Be Careful on What You Dream

Human beings are only performing naturally when striving to achieve some desirable goal and an integral part of continuous motivation is the constant drive to achieve. As Paul J. Meyer said: "Be careful on what you dream for it will inevitably come to pass." So what do you dream about?

Consider comedian Jay Leno. Long before he became famous, Leno says he always imagined himself doing comedy and enjoying luxury cars. His interest dates back to his teen years when he worked for a Rolls Royce dealer doing oil changes and picking up parts.

He recalls the difference in attitude between himself and his co-workers: "All the guys would say, 'Gee, wouldn't it be great to be the personal mechanic to some guy who had a collection of these cars?' And I just thought, 'Wouldn't it be great to be the guy?'"

Today, with a collection of 22 motorcycles and over a dozen high-priced antique and luxury cars, Leno is "the guy".

Writing Down Your Goals

When planning your goals, consider this simple piece of logic: if you aim at nothing, you will hit it every single time!

You will be amazed at the immediate difference in your motivation after you have set out your goals. Try it and see! A goal-setting action plan involves:

- Setting out realistic, achievable goals for every area of your life;
- Analysing the obstacles to overcome and actions required to achieve the goals;
- Setting target dates for the start and completion of each goal;
- Monitoring your progress;
- Giving yourself a reward for the attainment of your objectives.

SETTING GOALS

Goal to be Achieved	Start Date	Completion Date

Action steps required to achieve goal	Completed
1	
2	
3	
4	
5	
6	
7	
8	
9	
10	

How will progress be monitored (daily, weekly, monthly)? Write down the dates on which the goal was monitored and any corrective action required to assist you in the successful completion of your stated objectives.

Date monitored	Remarks	Date monitored	Remarks

Stop putting things off

Procrastination has been called the thief of time and we all fall into its trap at some time or other. The first step to banishing this destructive trait forever is to recognise the futility of it and to be ruthless in its elimination. It leads to frustration, anxiety and a host of unsolved problems that generally only get worse. As Denis Waitley once wrote:

> "Procrastination is the fear of success. People procrastinate because they are afraid of the success they know will result if they move ahead now. Because success is heavy and carries a responsibility with it, it is much easier to procrastinate and live on the "someday I'll" philosophy."

The motivation to be gained just from completing long overdue tasks can be considerable. To prove this point to yourself, list three tasks that you have been putting off, set a short-term timetable for their completion and start now!

1. ________ to be completed by ___/___/___
2. ________ to be completed by ___/___/___
3. ________ to be completed by ___/___/___

Your salespeople may put off writing quotations, making call-backs or checking out customer queries, with the result that orders, and tempers, are lost. This is merely habit and you need to resolve with determination to help them develop better ones. Always keep in mind this simple piece of logic: if you want to make an easy job seem hard, just keep putting off doing it.

Goal-setting action plan

There are five steps involved in goal setting:

1. Itemise (the master plan)
2. Categorise (putting them in order)
3. Prioritise (listing the priorities)
4. Visualise (pictures to feed motivation)
5. Realise (keeping a motivating record)

I have devised a series of templates for you to use or adapt for each of these steps, and they are shown on the following pages. First, here are some hints on filling in your goal-setting action plan:

- Your goals must be realistic. They should present a challenge but still be possible to attain. It is absolutely imperative that your goals are your own and are not unfairly influenced by people outside of your immediate family — or indeed within your family. It is, after all, your life, and sacrificing your desires for the sake of others will impact your motivation in a negative way.

- Next, you must really want whatever goals you decide on. Anything worthwhile usually involves hard work and goal-setting is no exception. You will need all your energy and motivation if things do not go according to plan. Developing the ability to picture vividly in your mind what it is you want will help you to achieve the end result.
- Having decided on the goal, analyse exactly what you have to do to achieve it. Anticipate the obstacles that you will inevitably have to overcome and, of course, what you're going to do to solve them.
- There must be start and finish dates. A football match without a time limit would be pointless and there would be no winner.
- The rewards to you on achievement are extremely important. List them in as much detail as possible. They will feed your motivation and urge you on to success.
- Your goals will obviously span different areas of you life — your career, your family life and your own development.

Writing down your goals helps to clarify your thinking and strengthens the commitment you are making with yourself. Fuzzy thoughts will produce fuzzy results. On the other hand, an organised plan will spur you into action and increase your determination to succeed. Allow your goals to be flexible. You will be a different person in five years' time and what you now think will make you happy may change. Take whatever time you need to fill them in — and do it now!

ITEMISE

Write down here everything you've ever wanted, every place you've wanted to go, and everything you'd like to become or achieve. Date each item when you enter it.

CATEGORISE

Separate goals into the appropriate categories as listed here. List each goal in probable order of priority

Personal Goals (Everything you ever wanted to achieve)
1.
2.
3.
4.
5.

Domestic and Family Goals (What the family would like to do together)
1.
2.
3.
4.
5.

Education Goals (Your future development)
1.
2.
3.
4.
5.

Career Goals (Position you would like to achieve)
1.
2.
3.
4.
5.

Repeat this exercise for every other area of personal importance, i.e. Physical, Recreational, Material, Spiritual and Financial. Do not limit yourself to the number of goals and keep adding to it month after month.

PRIORITISE

List here the three, five or ten things you have selected based on your high degree of desire. These are things to have, places to go, anything you want to become.

VISUALISE

Aids to Visualisation

Pictures, Photographs and other Symbols to help you visualise your goals.

REALISE	
Goals Achieved *As you achieve your goals, list them here. This will help to reinforce your confidence and motivation in setting others.*	
Goal Achieved:	Completion Date: / /
What it meant to me:	
Goal Achieved:	Completion Date: / /
What it meant to me:	
Goal Achieved:	Completion Date: / /
What it meant to me:	
Goal Achieved:	Completion Date: / /
What it meant to me:	

FURTHER YOUR OWN EDUCATION

The quickest way to become an old dog is to stop learning new tricks. Avoid ever getting to the stage when you think you have nothing left to learn. Far too many managers give the "impression" that they know all they need to know about selling. I can count on the fingers of one hand the number of sales managers I know who participated in a sales course and certainly never in a course about customer care. This attitude never ceases to amaze me because selling is changing almost daily and skills acceptable two years ago may no longer inspire people to buy your products. Where in the past we gave something free to get the customer's attention, nobody wants anything free anymore *unless* it adds value!

In furthering your own education:

- Have a look at the skills you need to develop. Buy books, do a course or visit other successful companies to see how their salespeople and managers operate.
- Talk to as many customers as you can and ask the hard question: What are we not doing that we should be doing?
- Form a co-op of other sales managers, meet once a month for the purpose of exchanging information and ideas.
- Appoint somebody to accumulate a library of information, manuals, magazines or anything that can be distributed to you and your salespeople to increase knowledge of the industry or specialised subjects.
- Draw up a training schedule for all staff members, including management, and get on the mailing list of all relevant bodies.
- Check out personal development organisations such as Toastmasters to further develop your ability to speak in public.

There are so many things a manager can do to improve motivation and as motivation is highly contagious, everybody will benefit. Lead with confidence and enthusiasm and your staff will surely follow.

SALES MANAGEMENT PERSONALITY TEST

All sales managers will have, to a lesser or greater extent, a combination of the following qualities, which can be summarised by the mnemonic PERSONAL SUCCESS SKILLS. Test yourself and see how well you do. Score yourself out of ten points on each attribute and tot up your scores on completion of the test.

- *Perseverance*. The ability to continue on your course of action despite difficulties or opposition. The efforts expended today are rarely reflected in today's results. You may have to revisit the same situation many times before you finally reap the rewards.

- *Empathy*. Probably the most important attribute in management — the ability to put yourself mentally in the other person's shoes. It is the skill of experiencing the other person's feelings and emotions imaginatively. Many people confuse empathy with sympathy, yet there is a distinct difference. Sympathy literally means to "be in favour of or agreement with one's mood or opinions", whereas empathy means to really understand, but not necessarily to agree. Empathy only becomes possible if you can mentally see the selling role from the salesperson's point of view. There is an old Spanish expression: "In order to be a bullfighter you must first learn to be a bull."
- *Resilience*. The ability to bounce back from disappointment and recover strength quickly. There will be many times when you get that "maybe I'm not cut out to be a sales manager" feeling. Just about every professional has uttered those words at some time or another. We need resilience to remind us that we are members of one of the most exciting and most frustrating professions in the world, and that every day will bring new opportunities and many disappointments. Thomas Edison suffered hundreds of failures before he finally invented the light bulb. In fact, many of the greatest inventions of our time would still be mere laboratory toys were it not for the resilience of their creators.
- *Sincerity*. Being genuine and honest without conceit or pretense — one of those qualities that are rarely faked with any success. Your sales team must have the confidence that you mean what you say and say what you mean.
- *Open mind*. An absence of prejudiced or narrow-minded views, it means allowing mental access to the opinions and views of others in an effort to learn from their experiences.

- *Neat appearance.* If you claim to work for a successful company with superior products, then you must dress in a manner that is consistent with your company's image. This also sends a message to your sales team that this is the way you want them to dress when visiting customers.
- *Ambition to succeed.* The burning desire to achieve your predetermined objectives. Ambition must be coupled with an active determination to achieve your personal and business goals. Talk to your sales team about the importance of setting goals — or better still, show them what goals have done for you.
- *Loyalty.* Being faithful to people you are under an obligation to defend or support. Salespeople find it refreshing to hear their manager speak well of their company and colleagues.
- *Self-confidence.* Our belief in our own abilities. If you tell yourself subconsciously you can't do something, you'll find in every case that you were right. "Skill and confidence," as an old proverb puts it, "are an unconquered army."
- *Understanding of human relations.* The human touch — showing kindness and consideration to other people. For sales managers, this means practicing and developing a combination of various skills, many of which will be discussed throughout this book.
- *Common sense.* The ability to absorb facts and learn from a new experience. All successful people are alert to opportunities to improve their performance. They aren't satisfied with today's results; they want to do better tomorrow. It also means being able to focus your strengths and efforts on the task in hand.
- *Co-operation.* Working together with your colleagues, subordinates and superiors as a team trying to achieve one common goal. Putting aside petty differences of opinion for the sake of the company objectives. Working with your

salespeople and your customers to build new levels of professionalism.

- *Enthusiasm*. The magic spark that gets support without ever having to ask for it. Not only is it contagious, it is also the greatest motivator known to man. It is the burning inner drive that helps us to persuade people without pressurising them. Emerson said that without enthusiasm nothing great was ever achieved.
- *Simplicity*. Speaking a language that others understand. Skills are useless unless you have the ability to communicate thoughts and ideas to others in a manner that is acceptable and easily understood.
- *Self-motivation*. This comes from developing a sincere desire for the things you want most out of life.
- *Sense of direction*. Devise a daily plan and daily targets and keep the benefits of your goals at the front of your mind all the time.
- *Knowledge*. Search constantly for more information about the marketplace and the trends of future months and years. Strive to perfect and update your team's selling skills, to improve sales presentations and increase orders.
- *Integrity*. Honourable standards of ethics and professionalism. Our profession operates to a set of accepted principles that must guide our conduct. Exercising a high standard of integrity will, at the very least, establish your credibility as a professional sales manager.
- *Listening ability*. In the history of selling, nobody ever listened themselves out of a sale. A winner listens, a loser just waits until it's his turn to talk. Joe Girard, the Detroit salesman who is credited in the *Guinness Book of Records* as "the world's greatest salesman", put it in a nutshell when he said "God gave us two ears and one tongue so we could listen

more than we talk." It was that philosophy that helped him sell 1,425 individual new cars in one year.

- *Leadership skills*. The ability to influence or direct your own course of action through your own efforts. We are either the masters or the victims of our destiny. Everybody has the option of being the passenger or the driver in his or her career.
- *Sense of humour*. The ability to appreciate or express amusement. Managing people is a serious business but we need to have the ability to introduce humour and the common sense to use it where appropriate.

As a guide to your self-analysis, seek the unbiased opinions of two others when completing the graph on the following page. What you may discover is that their view of you is quite different from the picture you have of yourself.

Tot up your marks and appraise yourself against these scores:

- 201 to 210: Give up your job immediately and apply for sainthood.
- 171 to 200: An outstanding score — be sure it is realistic.
- 141 to 170: This figure suggests great personal confidence.
- 111 to 140: This is an excellent score and indicates great integrity.
- 81 to 110: Indicates an amount of work to be done. High on humility.
- 00 to 80: Are you sure you are in the right job?

PERSONAL DEVELOPMENT GRAPH

	0	1	2	3	4	5	6	7	8	9	10
Perseverance											
Empathy											
Resilience											
Sincerity											
Open mind											
Neat appearance											
Ambition to succeed											
Loyalty											
Self-confidence											
Understanding of Human Relations											
Common sense											
Co-operation											
Enthusiasm											
Simplicity											
Self-motivation											
Sense of direction											
Knowledge											
Integrity											
Listening ability											
Leadership skills											
Sense of humour											
	0	1	2	3	4	5	6	7	8	9	10

Ten Key Points for Keeping Yourself Motivated

1. It is all right to forget your mistakes, provided you learn from their lessons.
2. Make the decision to be the best at whatever you do!
3. Practise what you cannot do. Think in terms of "that's the way I used to be . . ."
4. Don't try to reinvent the wheel; capitalise on the experience of others.
5. Use your imagination; see yourself as successful — not as a failure.
6. Remember, nobody can make you feel inferior without your consent.
7. Get into the habit of seeing the opportunities coming out of every problem.
8. Associate with positive people — avoid the prophets of doom and gloom.
9. Carry out a frequent mental overhaul — check what you think and say!
10. Be creative — allow mental access to the ideas and views of other people.

Chapter Three

Building Salespeople's Motivation

People motivation is a complex subject and impossible to cover in any comprehensive detail, but this should not prevent us addressing the main issues. No two people are alike and what motivates one may do nothing for another; what inspires enthusiastic activity today may cease to be a motivator tomorrow. This book is not intended as a panacea for all motivational problems but rather as a fundamental guide to managers anxious to improve morale, attitude and overall performance.

Of one thing you can be certain: if motivational problems prevail, there is every chance that the immediate manager is part of the problem. If you are part of the problem, then it stands to reason that you are also part of the solution.

Indirectly, salespeople wrote this chapter, because it is their views, their comments and their contributions which have had the biggest influence on the material you are about to read, and ultimately they are the only real experts on how they should be managed. Let us start by looking at all the factors that affect salespeople's motivation.

Motivational Factors

Compensation System

Salespeople will invariably compare their compensation package with rivals and if a disparity in earning exists, you have a potential motivational problem. "Inequity" — real or imagined — is difficult to deal with because salespeople like to think they are at least on a par with their opposite numbers in competitive organisations. Salespeople do join other companies for a better car or a bigger title and while these issues may appear unimportant, managers will ignore them at their peril.

In one company that I worked with as a consultant, the annual presentation of the salespeople's compensation package caused so much bad feeling, not only by the manner in which it was communicated, but also because the designer of the package had no understanding of how people sell. To compound the aggravation felt by the team, when salespeople expressed their dissatisfaction, they were advised to "take it or leave it" and many of the better people exercised that choice — and left.

The problem was that the compensation package was designed by the financial controller determined to keep costs down and presented by a manager who was clearly of the opinion that salespeople could never earn more than him. The net effect of this arrogant, penny-pinching stupidity was that the better salespeople left and those who stayed did so for one reason only — they were well past their sell-by date and unlikely to be employed by other companies. Is it any surprise that, in ten years of operation, this company never achieved a sales target or recorded a profit?

One of my most satisfying sales consultancy successes was to be able to reverse this unacceptable situation. Having gained the agreement of the chief executive that I would take responsibility for designing the compensation package, I spent many days trying to find a format that would work within the financial ceilings imposed on me by senior management.

Eventually, through trial and error, I came up with a system that rewarded those salespeople most capable of returning a top performance and without whose efforts we could not achieve our targets (see pages 138–9). Most important of all, I gave them three separate options and allowed them to make the choice on which system they wanted to employ. In spite of the fact that it was not a great package, they appreciated that I was genuinely trying to find a win-win solution: if they achieved targets, they would benefit through substantially increased earnings. They responded so well to this "combined" effort on compensation that for the first time in the company's history, they achieved target and made a profit.

Most of the excellent companies recognise that sales compensation should not be a motivational issue with the sales team. If they are not adequately rewarded, not only will you incur serious attitudinal problems, but your salespeople may also be tempted to bend the truth with customers in order to make up the deficit. Buyers who are victims of this unprofessional approach will never give your company the opportunity to repeat the experience. Managers who blindly follow this creed almost guarantee that the achievement of company sales targets will always be a constant struggle.

Relationship with Managers

Even for those with outstanding management skills, there are always daily motivational issues to address; but what chance has the manager who doesn't take time out to investigate his or her own motivational impact on the sales team? Salespeople consider the relationship with their immediate manager to have the most significant influence on their morale and motivation. While top sales managers inspire the team to maximum achievement, others provoke only a minimal response.

Activity

When salespeople were asked to list the areas they felt most negatively affected their motivation, the following were their top 20 answers. If a combination of these factors is in evidence, they can cause the most reasonable people to react in a negative manner. If this exercise is to have any value, it is essential to be honest in your appraisal. If any of these elements prevail, there is a good chance that your team motivation needs to be revisited.

Tick each box that you honestly believe applies to you or your management style and appraise your motivational influence according to the scoring system that follows the factors:

- ❑ Management failure to deliver on promises
- ❑ No opportunity for advancement or development
- ❑ Overuse of fear motivation — "improve or else"
- ❑ Lack of opportunity to offer opinions or influence events
- ❑ A belief that others are getting unfair or special treatment
- ❑ Bad-humoured managers
- ❑ Lack of interest in the individual needs of the sales force
- ❑ No recognition by management of a job well done
- ❑ A perception that salary is inadequate for effort expended
- ❑ Poorly communicated policy changes that affect salespeople personally
- ❑ Not knowing where one stands in the eyes of management
- ❑ Being chastised in front of staff or customers
- ❑ An imbalance of criticism over encouragement
- ❑ A feeling of being "talked down to"
- ❑ Unpleasant working environment
- ❑ A perceived "bad deal" compared against "conditions" within the industry
- ❑ A prevailing "us and them" attitude.
- ❑ Punishing staff for making "mistakes"
- ❑ Dissatisfaction with management attitude or manner
- ❑ Lack of trust, respect or confidence in management.

Scoring System:

0 to 4

If this is realistic, it is an excellent score and probably reflected in high levels of morale, motivation and the achievement of sales targets. If contrary to these scores you still have personnel problems, perhaps you should distribute the above list to your staff and invite them to complete them anonymously — you may get a few surprises!

5 to 9

Even top organisations have management/staff problem areas, so don't be too downhearted about your score. Console yourself in the knowledge that you are doing many of the right things, note the negative areas and work with determination towards their elimination.

10 to 14

This is a very honest appraisal but it also indicates very serious motivational difficulties. It is strongly recommended that you follow all the guidelines contained in this book. If all of these factors prevail, there is one certainty: management are definitely part of the problem!

15 plus

Provided you are not being overly critical, this score highlights the need for urgent remedial action. On the positive side, as you have identified where many of the problems are, solving them will be a lot easier. There is no doubt that in order to establish a new working spirit in the company, management will need to totally reappraise attitude, manner and conduct.

The Perceptual Gulf

What salespeople want from their job and what management *think* salespeople want from their job are frequently two different things. Here is a test I frequently use. Take a pencil and numerically rate the following, from one to ten, according to what you think is the order of importance to your salespeople, one being the most important and ten the least important:

- ☐ Possibility for promotion
- ☐ Feeling "in" on decisions
- ☐ Job security
- ☐ Help with personal problems
- ☐ Good compensation

- ❑ Interesting work
- ❑ Appreciation for a job well done
- ❑ Loyalty of management to staff
- ❑ Tactful discipline
- ❑ Good working conditions

Compare your ratings with those of other sales managers who have also taken this test; they said:

1. Good compensation
2. Job security
3. Good working conditions
4. Help with personal problems
5. Possibility for promotion
6. Interesting work
7. Appreciation for a job well done
8. Tactful discipline
9. Feeling "in" on decisions
10. Loyalty of management to staff.

If you agree with the majority, there is a good chance that you have also rated compensation as number one! Salespeople on the other hand, rarely, if ever, rate compensation any higher than *fourth*.

While staff ratings will vary from individual to individual, what never changes is how they collectively rate the most important motivator of all: appreciation for a job well done. Copy out the above headings and ask your salespeople individually to prioritise the list. There is a good chance that it will more closely resemble the following order, as selected by salespeople who have also taken this test:

1. Appreciation for a job well done
2. Feeling "in" on decisions
3. Interesting work
4. Good compensation
5. Loyalty of management to staff
6. Tactful discipline
7. Help with personal problems
8. Good working conditions
9. Possibility for promotion
10. Job security.

There really isn't a downside to carrying out this activity with your sales team. By doing so, you are sending a message to your people that you care about what they think and it will also alert you to any deficiencies in your current management style.

Any manager who wishes to improve staff performance should start by finding out exactly what it is that motivates each individual. Managers place too much emphasis on salary and job security when it is the human side of management that scores highest in practically every case.

Attitudes of Senior Management towards Salespeople

Attitudes within companies towards their own salespeople are changing, but not quickly enough. It is understandable that the traditional views have created unfair perceptions of today's "professional". Admittedly, there are salespeople whose ethics are questionable and these don't enhance the overall image of the sales profession. Because old-fashioned perceptions linger in the folk memory, the sales manager must effectively refute misconceptions by establishing the professional integrity of the modern-day salesperson.

As the sales manager, you may also have a major selling role in "selling" the sales team to senior management and giving them gentle reminders that they also have a significant supportive role to play. This can be in the form of a written acknowledgement of a top performance, offering positive encouragement at sales meetings or an occasional visit to salespeople in the field. As a salesperson, I can only ever recall one occasion where the chief executive graced me with his presence and it had a dual effect: I did a major spring-cleaning job on my sales materials and his visit inspired a boost of sustained motivation which kept me going for months!

Some time ago, I conducted a sales course where company-wide attitudes towards salespeople were anything but positive. At my instigation, the managing director persuaded senior managers to attend the course as "observers". On its completion, they conceded that selling was a much more difficult role than they had imagined and appreciated the amount of effort that went into getting a hearing, never mind an order. They were surprised too at the strong emphasis placed on "ethics", which came as a surprise to many. I have been assured the relationships between management and salespeople have improved considerably as a result of this experience.

Support from Other Departments

Few companies are in business just to make friends; the bottom line is higher profits. This will be achieved in one of three ways:

- Increase of profitable sales, including selling the same amount at a higher price;
- Reduced overheads or selling costs;
- A combination of both of the above.

The performance of the sales team will undoubtedly have the most significant influence on the achievement of these objectives. Why do so many companies fail to make the connection between active support for salespeople and the potential for higher sales and profits?

In competitive market conditions, even the most highly motivated salesperson is not guaranteed the business, so what chance has a salesperson who is under-motivated? Selling may be not be the most difficult job in the world but when a company's approach to the motivation factor is devoid of common sense, never mind innovative thinking, the whole sales effort is undermined needlessly.

I have observed the selling world from many angles and I am surprised at the lack of support by management and staff for the people whose selling capacities keep them in a job. The sales manager may have a more difficult role in motivating the sales team than is often apparent. An unhelpful receptionist, an insensitive account clerk or a moody senior manager can frustrate the efforts of the salespeople and undo all the sales manager's hard work.

The view of selling from within is often based on a lack of understanding of what the job involves and is probably not helped by what the staff observe when salespeople visit the office. As one non-sales manager once said, "Your people have a great job; they spend their time drinking coffee, making phone calls, swapping jokes and chatting up my staff." We should never forget that salespeople put up with a lot of "rejection" in the field and they need the occasional sanctuary of the office where they can recharge the batteries, feed off the motivation of colleagues and spend a little time with an encouraging sales manager. You may, however, need to make them sensitive to other staff when they are back at the office.

Harmony of All Relationships

Friction between sales and other departments is not unusual in companies. Communication is reduced to contact only by senior managers. Whatever the reasons, this lack of co-operation militates against the growth of a company. Successful companies thrive on inter-departmental communication.

Selling, no matter how effective, will have no long-term benefits for your company if there is not a high "customer care" awareness — enthusiastically demonstrated by salespeople and supported *throughout the organisation.* The importance of harmony between the departments will be discussed in greater detail in Chapter 10, "The Enemy Within".

WIN-WIN: A FORMULA FOR SUCCESSFUL SALES MANAGEMENT

The number of books written on motivation would fill the shelves of any library. Yet if managers were to understand, practise and apply the principles of win-win communication, teamwork and staff morale would improve almost immediately.

These principles, outlined in Chapter 1, when applied to the sales process itself, involve building a long-term relationship with buyers, based not on manipulation but on the establishment of a mutual understanding. In contrast to the single-minded, blinkered approach of using manipulative techniques to close a sale, first time, no matter what, win-win uses this mutual understanding to establish the genuine needs of the buyer, so that the salesperson can attempt to match these needs with the product or service their company is offering.

The sales manager can use these same win-win principles to motivate his or her sales team. In this case, the mutual understanding created between manager and salesforce involves investigating, through open communication, what can be done to meet the needs of everybody involved: the manager, the salespeople, the organisation and the customer. If you could introduce the spirit of win-win into everything you do — communicating with salespeople, dealing with fellow managers, handling difficult customers and all other forms of human interaction — not only will you increase motivation, you will also increase sales and profits.

In order for these skills to work, a number of factors must apply:

- There must be recognition that if management behaviour or attitude is causing motivational problems, only a change of management behaviour or attitude will resolve them.

- Managers cannot be selective as to how, or to whom, they apply these skills. Any "relics" from past disputes or disagreements should be forgotten. Harbouring resentment towards any individual, however justified, only serves to dilute the spirit of the exercise.
- As the bottom line is to improve motivation, managers must be prepared to cross over the divide between being "right" and doing the "right thing". A manager may be "right" to confront a staff member for being late for work, but the "right thing" is not to mention it until that person has completed the day's activities.

The win-win approach and its impact on motivation is only common sense, but it is only common sense when somebody points it out to you. This crucial part of human interaction is so often taken for granted; yet managers who practise what they preach will create a higher level of positive rapport with salespeople and achieve greater job satisfaction into the bargain.

Before looking in detail at the motivational aspects of win-win management, let us look at the alternatives.

Consider the Downside of all other Options

In order to appreciate the significance of win-win, let us first look at more common but less favourable options. Stephen Covey, in his excellent book *The 7 Habits of Highly Effective People*, outlines them as:

- Win-Lose or Lose-Win
- Lose-Lose.

More favourable methods are:

- Win-Win or No Deal
- Win-Win.

Win-Lose or Lose-Win — How to Inspire People to Give the Minimum

These two headings are combined because they are inextricably interlinked. People who follow the creed of win-lose will themselves become a victim of the reverse: lose-win. As mentioned earlier, the manager who confronts a staff member for being late (I win/you lose) may cause that person to be demotivated for the rest of the day (You win/I lose).

The win-lose mentality is the root cause of most motivational problems. It destroys relationships, encourages reprisals, discourages teamwork and eventually breaks the spirit of the most enterprising people.

A few years ago, I sat in a manager's office and listened in horror as I overheard him angrily humiliate one of his staff for arriving late for work. He used words like:

"I am tired of this . . ."

"Last chance . . ."

"Poor example to others . . ."

"Constantly letting me down . . ."

This is an example of the win-lose personality and a scenario most of us have witnessed. This person was at the front line of customer service and one can only imagine her attitude to her job for the remainder of the day — not to mention what she had to say about her boss at the staff coffee break. He may have won the battle, but he lost the war!

Later, he discovered that he had nobody to work late that evening as two people were on leave and one staff member was ill. He called in the woman who was on her "last chance" and asked if she would help him out that evening. She replied: "I have made other plans that I cannot alter at such short notice." I subsequently discovered that this was not true.

This only serves to reinforce the point that if people suffer from a win-lose mentality, it may take time, but "victims" will eventually get their revenge! Many organisations rely on the positive support of their suppliers, yet when the lose-win personality suffers poor service, he writes:

> "I cannot believe you could possibly employ such stupid people."
>
> "I am writing to you to tell you how I feel about your dreadful service."
>
> "Your staff have caused me enormous embarrassment."

These letters usually conclude with threats of taking the business elsewhere or demands for compensation. This attitude only inspires suppliers to give the minimum and salespeople who are victims of this approach will also do the absolute minimum required to keep their job.

Lose-Lose — A Recipe for War!

Lose-lose is a belief in total destruction and, as we all know, the legal profession makes a substantial part of their living on the back of this mentality.

In a highly acrimonious divorce, the judge ordered a man to split all the family assets down the middle with his wife. As a disciple of the creed of "get even", his first stop on the way home was to the local hardware store to hire a chainsaw. We can only guess at the perverted pleasure he experienced as he systematically cut his way through every piece of furniture they possessed.

I recall a classic lose-lose situation involving a sales manager and one of his sales team. Mike, an excellent salesperson, was capable of achieving his year's quota in six months, was everybody's tip for promotion and was a firm favourite with customers and colleagues.

On this occasion, he was experiencing a tough selling patch and his downturn in motivation was probably a direct reflection of other things that were going on in his personal life. As it was just a small sales team, Mike's non-performance was always likely to cause the sales manager to come under pressure from the Chief Executive.

Of all the people I have worked with, Mike's sales manager has had the biggest influence on my own development as a manager — in two years, I learned how *not* to handle salespeople. He was a selfish, insensitive individual with his sights clearly focused on moving quickly up the promotion ladder — regardless of cost or inconvenience to others. Mike's non-performance was beginning to tarnish the sales manager's profile and something had to be done.

The sales manager decided to tackle Mike on his poor selling performance. Mike, in what he described as a plea for help, explained that he was so de-motivated that he was unable to face his customers for the past few days and, in fact, he had stayed at home. When questioned as to how he got over the problem of providing a call report (which every salesperson had to provide), he explained that while he had listed the calls in his report, he hadn't actually made the calls. To his surprise, the sales manager was supportive and empathetic and as Mike left the meeting he was determined to "get out and do what he was paid to do".

The following day, Mike received a letter in the post from the sales manager, which read as follows:

> Dear Mike,
>
> Copy: Chief Executive/General Manager
>
> As you know, we have had lengthy discussions about your present sales performance and at our meeting yesterday you assured me that you were making every effort to achieve your quota.
>
> Subsequent to our meeting, I took a full day out of my busy schedule to check your daily sales reports and personally called on companies where you claimed to have made a visit. I was disappointed to note that not one of the contacts listed had any knowledge of any meeting having taken place between you and them.

> It is disappointing that when we need our salespeople to be pulling their weight, you should choose to find other things to be doing with your time.
>
> This is a most serious breach of company policy and if it reoccurs, you will be suspended without pay.

When Mike received the letter, he wrote this reply:

> Dear Sales Manager,
>
> Copy: Chief Executive/General Manager
>
> You have a rather jaundiced view of our meeting. Contrary to claiming that I was putting in the effort, I readily admitted that the situation was the direct opposite and why you should claim otherwise baffles me. I told you I had not been working that day so why the cloak-and-dagger investigation into my sales calls?
>
> Perhaps you can explain to the people you copied with your note, how you were able to talk to contacts listed on my daily sales reports — which was made up of people who don't actually exist. Whatever you may say about your busy schedule, your time was certainly not lost on my territory.
>
> It will not be necessary for you to suspend me as I am terminating my association with the company forthwith.

The result: Mike moved on and the sales manager lost his job. Extreme example? Thankfully yes, but it does make an important point about the lose-lose mentality, summed up in this grave piece of wisdom:

> Here lies the body of William Jay
> Who died maintaining his right of way
> He was right, dead right as he sped along
> But he is just as dead as if he were wrong!

Win-Win or No Deal — A formula for contracts of employment!

This concept is frequently becoming a feature of contracts of employment, where both parties agree the basis for the working relationship and unless both are satisfied, there is no deal. It can be used thus:

> "This is your contract of employment; it outlines in detail the important aspects of your role. It also explains what we can expect from each other. If you are satisfied with the contents please sign it and return it to me. If you are unhappy with any aspect of the document and subsequently it cannot be explained to your total satisfaction, I would prefer that you did not take the job!"

This concept and approach would save everybody a lot of grief — provided both parties stick rigidly to the original agreement.

Win-Win — Motivating People to Peak Achievement

It may not always be possible to achieve, but a win-win approach should be the ultimate aim of all our communication with others. As Stephen Covey says in *The 7 Habits of Highly Successful People*:

> Win/Win is a frame of mind and heart that constantly seeks mutual benefit in all human interaction. Win/Win means that agreements or solutions are mutually beneficial, mutually satisfying.

The motivation of win-win people is based on their understanding of what this frame of mind can achieve:

- It helps us to create a co-operative rather than a competitive working environment;
- It is not my way or your way — it is *our* way;
- That all solutions and agreements will be *mutually beneficial*;
- That all parties feel positively committed to the action plan.

People who follow the creed of win-win think in terms of: "how can I communicate this in such a way as to encourage the other person to respond in a positive manner and ensure both of us benefit?"

Win-win managers who want to improve timekeeping would probably say something like:

> "Because you are such a valuable member of my team and because other staff members look to you for your example, we need to discuss ways of improving your timekeeping."

A thorough understanding of the principles of win-win can help to improve motivation in the workplace, increase professionalism in business and create a more harmonious relationship with loved ones.

WIN-WIN MANAGEMENT

Have a look at the following list of management traits and decide on which method is likely to yield the most positive response from staff:

The Win-Lose Manager	**The Win-Win Manager**
Demands respect	Earns respect
Wants to be right	Wants to do the right thing
Wants to be admired	Wants to be believed
Punishes publicly	Calmly corrects in private
Points out faults	Highlights strengths
Condemns and criticises	Encourages new effort
Monopolises the talking	Monopolises the listening
Knows it all	Never stops learning
Talks to impress	Talks to express
Talks at staff	Talks with staff
Lectures and instructs	Shows by example
Displays authority	Displays humility
Destroys confidence and morale	Builds the desire to succeed

If managers cannot inspire staff to talk to them, if there is a penalty for holding unpopular views, then management will only be told what they want to hear. In these circumstances, neither the manager nor the staff will develop.

Aggression is one of the traits that suits nobody and is offensive to absolutely everybody. It may have some virtues on the battlefield but in a retail store or at a sales meeting it has none. The Chinese have a saying: "If a man sows beans he will reap beans." If a man sows aggression he will reap aggression. If somebody is polite and courteous to you, there is an obligation on your part to respond in like manner. If your management style includes any of the win-lose personality traits listed above, it is highly recommended that you work towards their elimination. Positive teamwork, motivation and a healthy working environment can only come about by practising positive win-win management. Chapter 4 looks at the positive management skills needed to create a healthy working environment.

Changing Attitudes

If you want people to change the way they do things, you must first bring about a change of attitude. Telling an individual that they must "change their ways" will only reinforce their resistance. Recognise that *practically all* attitudinal problems have their roots in a lack of personal confidence. These people need positive encouragement and a boost to their morale, not regular confirmation of their inadequacies.

There are usually only five reasons why people have attitudinal problems:

1. As a direct result of management attitude, behaviour and conduct towards staff (real or imagined);
2. Because the job falls well below "expectations" — it is "just a job" and unlikely to lead to a career;

3. Because individuals have no positive goals to achieve — no penalty for failure, no reward for success;
4. Personal circumstances, poor health, worry, and lack of goals, financial problems or other domestic difficulties;
5. Because the individual concerned is seriously lacking in personal confidence.

Because it is always easier to be negative than positive, negative people in a negative environment with negative motivation are recipes for poison, which if unchecked will eventually eat into the atmosphere. Even the most positive spirited individual will require enormous strength of character to maintain any level of enthusiasm in such surroundings.

Of all the skills a sales manager needs, it is the ability to bring about a change of attitude that is the most vital. One thing I can promise you is that these skills work. Over the years I have had to deal with some tough cookies and the skills I discuss below have never failed me. Throughout my years in attitudinal training I have come to some important conclusions, based not on opinions but experience:

- Practically all attitudinal problems have their roots in some "perceived" personal deficiency.
- I have never met a person whose attitude could not be improved dramatically, although some may require a little more help and time than others.
- When negative-thinking people do change their attitudes, the change tends to last for a long time and they frequently become the top salespeople in the company.

Many managers don't accept that it is part of their job to alter attitudes and can often be heard to say; "I am under enough pressure to get sales without people working against me." While this is quite an understandable reaction, it does not address the fundamental problem. If you can accept the suggestion that this individual is suffering from a serious lack of personal confidence, then you must also accept that managers usually go the wrong way in trying to bring about a change. This is how it normally happens: after several heated discussions, the manager, in frustration, resorts to:

- Saying things like, "you had better change your ways";
- Force, reprimand, threats and sometimes profanity;
- Pointing out where the offender's faults will lead;
- Showing up the salesperson in front of colleagues;
- Treating the offender differently from others.

Bearing in mind that the salesperson is possibly already in the depths of despair, one can see immediately what little chance there is in a sudden change of attitude. It takes a lot of humility to admit you are wrong and significantly, it is not a quality found in any great abundance by people lacking in personal confidence, so don't expect too much in the way of "I admit I have a problem." It is much too early for that!

> "You can't teach an old dog new tricks."
>
> "You can't change the habits of a lifetime."
>
> "You can bring a horse to the well but you can't make him drink."

These are often the encouraging words used by managers when outlining the trainee profile for a training programme. Yet none of these statements should ever find refuge in the mind of the successful manager. The secret to changing attitudes lies in a common-sense approach; you will have no problem bringing a horse to the well *and* getting him to drink — if you begin by making him thirsty!

What Motivates People to Change Their Attitudes?

While many people recognise the need for change, adults, unlike children, must be motivated to learn. They will learn and change only what they want, and only when it is perceived as being of some personal benefit. As attitudes are always influenced by past experiences, the motivation to change will be influenced by the level of desire to achieve important new goals. Once the individual is sold on the merits of goal achievement, there will also be a corresponding change of attitude.

Whatever adults learn they must learn for themselves; nobody can learn for them. Trying to "impose" change on an individual without his or her consent will fail. Attitudes are only a frame of mind: change the frame of mind and the attitude will change automatically. Instead of investing negative energy in explaining where a bad attitude will lead, outline the benefits of a new style of thinking.

It has been my experience that negative attitudes cannot be maintained in the face of outstanding patience and courtesy.

Tips on Changing Attitudes

- Don't allow anybody to infect you with prejudiced views on any individual and give people every opportunity to show their best side. This allows you to deal with individuals with an open mind.
- Remember that you are not dealing with a negative person; you are dealing with a confidence problem. Never draw reference to the fact that they are different in any way to other salespeople.
- Be polite, persistent and pleasant. Demonstrate by your manner that you do not intend to make him or her suffer because of their "unhelpful" manner. Many human qualities are contagious and it is difficult not to be influenced by a positive and courteous manager.

- Separate behaviour from personality; all too often they are confused. If you don't like his manner, recognise that this is no reason to dislike him as a person. Would you throw out your TV because you are getting a poor reception on one channel?

One of the best ways to improve a salesperson's attitude is to project a good one yourself. Difficult as it may be, try extra hard to find his or her better qualities. You can be certain that these qualities are there and you may also be the first person who ever noticed (in fact you probably will). If you can find these better traits and draw then out, your attitudinal problems are on the way to being resolved.

The Need for Self-analysis

One thing staff find irresistible in management is humility — having the ability to admit that you have made mistakes is not a sign of weakness but of great strength. If a manager accepts that he or she is partly responsible for a negative working environment, following some simple guidelines could increase motivation almost immediately:

- Call a staff meeting;
- Outline your concern about your personal impact on their motivation;
- Get a flipchart and write up a heading: "What should management do to increase staff motivation?";
- As the purpose of the exercise is only to get information and encourage people to participate, it is essential that your body language is not communicating agitation or annoyance.

From this meeting, you will begin to establish a new relationship with staff, built on trust and mutual respect, and you may be pleasantly surprised that it only requires "minor" concessions on your part to make a huge difference to their motivation. You will also have the opportunity of saying: "I will do this for you if you will do this for me." As staff/management attitudes are contagious, if you are reasonable in attitude they will also be reasonable in attitude.

Don't be overly concerned about not getting contributions from everybody; some people will need time to be convinced that the exercise is genuine. Once you put some of their requests into operation, they will realise that you do mean business and you will receive more positive input at subsequent meetings.

Help Staff with Personal Goals

There is an old saying: "A person going nowhere usually gets there." This is a crucial part of motivational management and you can significantly improve performance by encouraging staff to set and attain realistic personal goals. The root cause of most motivational problems is stagnation and a manager can change that overnight by helping people to "kick start" their further development. By doing so, you will not only help the individual but you will also benefit from their "new skills".

Unlike individuals, companies can put staff through night school or distance learning courses and receive grants and tax relief. Whether you see it as an "investment" or an "expense" is a very private matter, but nothing lifts motivation more quickly than an opportunity to grow with the business.

Set Team Development Goals

Teamwork divides the task and doubles the chances of success. Whenever managers delegate responsibility to individuals, they are also making an important statement — "I trust you and your judgement" — almost guaranteed to elicit a highly positive response. One of the greatest risks in business is *not* to take any risks and if you are not prepared to share responsibility you may as well do everything yourself.

There are many team goals that a sales manager can introduce which will not only assist in the achievement of sales targets but also create an atmosphere of "we are all in this together". Individuals could be delegated to:

- Research competitive activities;
- Design better customer proposals;
- Write more effective mail shots;
- Research a project of interest to all colleagues.

How to set team goals:

- Write up a master list and, where possible, delegate an "agreed" role to every individual.
- Ask each staff member to write up their own action plan as to how they will achieve their goal.
- Take time out to discuss and agree each individual action plan.
- Try and get them to share in the production of the ideas related to their goals — goal "ownership" will usually inspire a greater level of personal effort.
- Be absolutely certain that *both* parties understand, agree and accept that the goals are attainable. Review any problems they may encounter along the way.
- One of the most important aspects of goal achievement is "conviction". Reassure each individual that you have confidence in their ability, skill and knowledge to deliver on the objectives.
- Agree a start and finish date and how progress will be monitored.

Like everything else, management attitude to the success of this exercise is critical. Your role is to assist and encourage, not dominate or unfairly influence how each goal is achieved. If there is a bonus for the achievement of the objectives, this should be explained in clear terms. Most important of all, if an individual or collective incentive is agreed and the goal is achieved, the rewards must be delivered when expected.

The ultimate in motivation is to come up with a new idea and to have it acted on by management. It has been said that in the space of a career, the average Japanese employee will offer 3,000 ideas to management and few would dispute that they encourage a culture of creative innovation. Encourage this spirit of creativity, reward and give recognition for all new ideas implemented.

Ten Key Points from Building Salespeople's Motivation

1. Remember that what inspires enthusiastic selling activity today may cease to be a motivator tomorrow — keep in touch with your salespeople's changing needs.

2. If motivational problems prevail and you are part of the problem, it stands to reason that you must also be part of the solution.

3. Sales managers place too much emphasis on salary and job security when it is the human side of management that scores highest with salespeople in practically every case!

4. Make the decision now to start applying the principles of win-win to every aspect of your management style — start learning how to build a co-operative rather than a competitive working environment.

5. If you want people to change the way they do things, you first need to bring about a change of attitude. Telling people that they must "change their ways" will only reinforce their resistance. These people need encouragement, not regular confirmation of their inadequacies.

6. Practically all attitudinal problems have their roots in some perceived personal deficiency. Help people with the defi-

ciency and you automatically help them to alter their attitude.

7. Remember that adults, unlike children, will learn only what they want to learn and only when it is perceived as being of some personal benefit!
8. One of the best ways to change people's attitudes is to project a good one yourself.
9. You will significantly improve salespeople's performance if you can help and encourage them to set and attain realistic goals.
10. The ultimate for salespeople is to have their ideas acted on by management. Encourage this spirit of creativity. Be generous in your praise. Reward and give recognition.

Chapter Four

Creating a Positive Working Environment

Having discussed motivation, let us turn our attention to what needs to be done to sustain it. Success is a journey, not a destination, and to move motivational levels from where they are now to where you want them to be may take time. By applying these concepts you can expect an upturn in motivational levels, provided you make any required changes to your management style. Yes, there may be risks, but take heed of some excellent advice from Beverly Sills: "You may be disappointed if you fail but you are doomed if you don't try!"

My experience indicates that salespeople sell and work better in a friendly and positive sales office environment — the creation of which is the responsibility of management — if only because motivation is dependent on the quality of leadership.

Too many people incorrectly assume that because they hold exalted positions, the respect of others is automatic; this is certainly not the case. We respect others because of an admirable quality and in the case of a sales manager, this might be:

- Integrity — not tampering with the truth;
- Never backing out of a commitment — regardless of cost or inconvenience;
- A readiness to straighten out misunderstandings;
- Genuine interest in all salespeople and their problems;
- An ability to be fair and impartial in decisions;

- Being open-minded enough to learn, even from subordinates;
- Taking the responsibility but always being anxious to share the credit;
- A reputation for not holding grudges or having a "selective" memory;
- Ability to create and listen to new ideas.

People generate respect for others on the basis of what they *do* — not because of what they *are*. In the immortal words of Harold S. Geneen, the legendary leader of ITT:

> It is an immutable law in business that words are words, explanations are explanations, promises are promises, but only performance is reality.

Positive Management

You are the manager and you are the message, so try to develop the habit of talking with your people in a friendly and encouraging manner. Your people will follow your example not only in how they should communicate with you, but also in how they should communicate with each other.

Even the world's greatest communicators will almost certainly encounter sporadic moments of frustration and anger and how we handle them influences not only the resolution of the problem, but our continuing relationship with the offender. It is human to want to "let off steam" but we must not lose sight of the objective, which is to *resolve* the problem. Conflict will take place at any time and in the worst possible circumstances and it is good management to mentally practise your response to these moments in advance. It is simple:

- Never try to handle a difficult situation when you are upset or angry. If you do you will only make a bad situation worse.

- Revisit the situation after you have calmed down, in private and at a time of your choosing.
- Give win-win reasons for bringing the situation to the other person's attention and always try to start with positives. For example, "because I value our relationship" or "because you are such an important member of my team" is more likely to create a positive listening environment.
- Explain — *do not complain*. Avoid making judgements or personalising your remarks. Try to explain objectively and calmly exactly what you perceive the problem to be.

Of course, how we perceive others and where they fit into our "social and commercial network" has a significant influence on our ability to resolve disputes. Invariably, we see others as fitting into any one of five groups: those we see as seniors, juniors, equals, opponents and friends.

On one occasion, I was in consultation with a sales manager when we were politely interrupted by one of his salespeople. The manager used words like, "Can't you see I'm busy?" and "Can't this wait?" Somewhat exasperated, he left the room to deal with the salesperson's query. Five minutes later, we were interrupted once again by the chief executive who enquired, "Am I interrupting you?" at which the manager replied "No not at all, come right in, it would be great to get your input." We all understand his courteous reaction to the chief executive, but where is the justification for treating salespeople differently?

When we communicate with people senior in rank, our body language tends to be subservient, our manner takes on an air of diplomacy and our words are carefully chosen, and yet when we talk with subordinates, our communication tone tends to be the exact opposite. When people's views differ from ours we look on them as opponents and subconsciously try to "better" their argument.

However, when we view subordinates as friends, our demeanour tends to be more consistent with the spirit of win-win.

We talk politely and listen actively and there are no social or commercial barriers to poison the atmosphere. If we can achieve a friend-to-friend style of communication with all our contacts, particularly salespeople, we will create a climate of teamwork that makes positive outcomes a near certainty.

PHRASES TO AVOID

Another dimension to maintaining a friend-to-friend management style involves the avoidance of certain phrases almost guaranteed to offend your salespeople. Usually these statements are accompanied by controlled but aggressive body language, the combination of which sends a signal to the receiver — let's get ready for battle.

- *With all due respects*. (Interpretation: Thinking very little of you as I do . . .) There really isn't an alternative to this statement and while "with respects" is less offensive, you are still swimming in dangerous waters.
- *I disagree with you; You are entitled to your opinion*. (You are wrong!) As the purpose of most communication is to persuade others to consider your point of view, the best way to get people to accept your position is to accept that their opinion is also valid. Give people credit for their opinions and they are honour-bound to give you credit for yours.
- *To put this in simple terms; I hope this doesn't go over your head*. (You are such a fool that I am going to explain this to you in baby talk.) I witnessed a tutor lose the support of his students by saying: "Just to ensure that this session doesn't go over your heads . . ."
- *You have misinterpreted me*. (There was nothing wrong with the way I explained myself; you are the problem here and if only you were capable of better listening.) Try something like, "I have not explained myself properly."
- *If I were you; Think about what I said; My advice would be; If you want my opinion; I think what you should do is . . .* (You

are obviously not capable of making up your own mind so I will have to make it up for you.) Changing "I think" to "what do you think" could be the difference between succeeding and failing to get over your message. Similarly, "may I suggest . . ." is much easier on the ear than "my advice would be . . .".

- *I am not interrupting you . . . but . . .* (Shut up! What I have got to say is much more important.) We all do it and we know that it demonstrates very bad manners.
- *Now don't take offence . . . but; Don't take this personally . . . but . . .* (I am just about to verbally attack you.) Better to avoid it altogether.
- *So what you are trying to say is . . .* (You are obviously having problems trying to express yourself so I will do it for you.) What might sound better is "So in other words . . ."
- *I have a better idea* (Your idea wasn't much use, was it?) Perhaps use, "as an extension to your idea . . .".
- *I hope I am not boring you! Without boring you any further.* (I am bored by it, everybody else is bored by it.) This is an interesting one because when people use this phrase, listeners nearly always starts yawning. It has the same effect as "Don't think about a white horse." Avoid it altogether.
- *I am not condemning; I am not criticising; I am not complaining . . . but . . .* (That is precisely what I am about to do.)

If you want to destroy people, the selling atmosphere, your relationships with loved ones and fail big time as a manager, just master the habit of criticising, condemning and complaining. The use of any of these phrases is guaranteed to create tension, anger, resentment, retaliation and a highly contagious negative environment. A simple change of approach from "this is not a criticism" to "may I make an observation" can make a world of difference to how receptive people will be to your message.

Applying these skills is a lot easier than it seems and when you consider the perils of doing it any other way, your motivation to practise it will increase.

Develop Professional Management Skills

Whenever managers are asked to define their job, the most popular response is: *"To ensure that my department returns a profit."* When followed up with a second question, such as "And how is that achieved?", the answer is probably, *"By making sure that staff do the job they are paid to do."*

If *the* root cause of motivational problems could be identified, it is probably to be found in that response. This poorly thought out management attitude practically forces some to see their role as finding fault, criticising performance, dishing out instructions and keeping people on their toes — all the usual ingredients for a poisonous selling atmosphere.

Positive management, on the other hand, is a combination of:

- Recognising that the role of management is to *motivate staff to high levels of performance,* not just to make sure that staff *do their job* — and there is a difference!
- A clear understanding that money as a motivator has only limited value and that the level of "on-the-job" motivation is a direct reflection of management/staff relations.
- Explaining not only the "what" and "how" but also the "why" — knowing that this will help build purpose and enthusiasm for any given task.
- Recognising that salespeople are also customers of management and like any other customer they like to think that you care about them.
- Helping people to see the bigger picture of which they play a part, to see how their work and their contribution relates to the total package — service, sales and profits.

- Ensuring that management behaviour induces improvement, progress, achievement and challenge.
- Understanding and demonstrating that managers also see themselves as *members of the team* — prepared to support and lead by example.
- Always being available to staff for help and continual guidance, setting aside time, as a matter of routine, for properly prepared consultation.

Dale Carnegie said: "You can make more friends in two months by becoming really interested in them than you can in two years trying to get them interested in you." I recall that there is some useful advice for managers in the Bible, which tells us that "the measure you give will be the measure you get".

Admit Your Mistakes

Taking responsibility is an important management skill. Passing the buck or cries of "it's not my fault" are common and guaranteed to totally frustrate a listener. Having the courtesy to say "I'm sorry, I was wrong" or "It was entirely my fault" is a sign of strength and an admirable quality in sales managers whose humility will be remembered long after the mistake has been forgotten. Mistakes are a valuable experience, provided you learn from their lessons.

A number of years ago, I was addressing the sales team. A heated debate developed between Neil, one of the salespeople, and myself resulting in me accusing him of sending in his reports later than required. He left the office very angry, still protesting his innocence, but I was comforted in the knowledge that I had the evidence from the postmarks on his reports.

Later that day, my secretary informed me she had given me incorrect information and the salesperson in question had sent his reports exactly as he claimed. This incident occupied my thoughts for the entire weekend. Having considered the options, at our next sales meeting I directed my comments to Neil:

> "On Friday morning, I accused you of misrepresenting the situation as I believed it to be — it now transpires that you were right and I was wrong and as I accused you in front of your colleagues I would now like to apologise in front of your colleagues."

Years later he came to me and said that of all the incidents that had taken place in his time in the company, that was the most notable. Not only had it done a lot for our relationship, but also the anger he felt on coming in to work was replaced with a burst of sustained motivation.

The Power of Encouragement

Recognition serves as the greatest means of encouragement. We would never have heard of Charles Dickens but for the encouraging words of his first publisher. Another famous author was on the verge of suicide when his teacher told him he had a talent for writing: his name was H.G. Wells. Consider the power of these statements:

> "You really did a great job."
>
> "You have a very special talent for this kind of work."
>
> "I am delighted we are working together on this."
>
> "I appreciate all your efforts."
>
> "It's great to have you on the team."

Any manager who can demonstrate genuine appreciation for improvement-conscious staff will increase job satisfaction significantly. It is a powerful motivator; it is better than money and a lot less expensive. Writing a special note to a customer to thank him or her for the business can do much to maintain a positive relationship. Thanking a staff member for special effort will be noted with enthusiasm. Showing appreciation to loved ones for their patience and support can help to sustain much-needed personal motivation.

BRING STAFF INTO THE DECISION-MAKING PROCESS

The real experts on motivating your salespeople are your salespeople. You may learn a lot by seeking their opinions and comments. Among the most powerful statements are:

> "May I ask your advice on an idea that I am working on?"
>
> "I would really appreciate your views."
>
> "What is your opinion?"

It is remarkable what people achieve just by asking for opinions and advice. Asking a customer for his or her opinion on a new product coming out on the market may help build a new relationship. By seeking the opinions of staff, we make them feel important, reinforce their self-esteem and motivate them for days — all for the price of an opinion.

I recall, with some sadness, a senior salesperson telling me he had worked in his company for 25 years and never once had he been asked for an opinion. As he said, "Perhaps I didn't have a lot to offer, but it would have cost them nothing to find out." We all make the mistake of thinking that subordinates have little to contribute to management problems and the obvious thing to do is to call in the "experts". Sometimes the solution is so simple that it requires people removed from the problem to find it!

Many years ago, the El Cortez Hotel in San Diego came across a serious problem: the one elevator they had was incapable of handling the increasing numbers of people going through the hotel. They brought in architects, engineers, lift manufacturers and experts from all over the world. Eventually they found a solution: they decided to install another lift and thus planned to cut a hole in each floor from the basement right up to the penthouse. This would be a monumental task at enormous cost and major disruption to hotel traffic.

As the architects stood in the lobby discussing the plans, the janitor observed the proceedings and enquired what they proposed to do. When they explained the plan, he shook his head and said, "So you are going to close the hotel, make an almighty mess of the structure, reduce the accommodation and put me out of work?" In a poor attempt at humour, they asked him what he would do if it were up to him. He replied, "I'd build the elevator on the outside of the hotel!" The result: the El Cortez Hotel became the first structure in history to have an elevator on the outside of the building.

Opinions cost you nothing and can do so much for salespeople's morale and your own education. Why not also consider contacting former staff and asking for their opinions on how things could have been improved. As their job is not a risk, you may get more objective comments about your management style and your operation.

Reflective Activity

You must also be prepared to look to yourself and do some in-depth soul-searching. If your attitude, management style and behaviour is aggravating motivational problems, nothing will change until you make adjustments to your management style. Answer the following questions as honestly as you can:

- Would I like to have me as a boss?
- Would I like to have me as a member of staff?
- Would I like to have me as a spouse?
- Would I like to have me as a friend?
- Would I like to have me as a parent?
- Do I usually come in to work in good humour?
- Am I always encouraging in my comments to salespeople?
- Do I project a friendly style of communication?
- Do I congratulate staff on a job well done?

There are many other questions that can be asked but these are fundamental to people's motivation. If you have answered "no", "sometimes" or "depends" to any of these questions, and you have a few motivational problems, you can be sure of one thing— you *are* definitely part of the problem! Of course, the ultimate test is: How often do you sneak around the office in the hope of catching somebody doing something "right"?

A Pleasant Facial Expression

In my early selling days, I can recall looking at the early morning expression on the manager's face and thinking "It's going to be a good day" or "It's going to be a bad day". That probably sums up the influence the manager's facial expression can have on salespeople's morale. A manager unable to smile will do more to damage morale than any other circumstance. Facial expression tends to be habitual; we form habits and then the habits form us. One way to guarantee a friendlier demeanour is to replace negative thoughts with more pleasant positive mental images. When you accept that a new expression can increase sales performance, your motivation to smile more often will also increase. Look at it this way: all your salespeople will have their day brightened or darkened by the tone and manner of your greeting.

It was Confucius who said: "The man without a smiling face should not open a sweet shop." Considering it takes more muscles to frown than it does to smile, it is a wonder that we don't smile more often. One outstandingly successful Irish company has a definite policy on interviewing: if the interviewee does not smile as they walk into the room, they will not get the job! They work on the principle that if you have problems smiling, you have no business talking to their customers.

WORK HARDER AT REMEMBERING PEOPLE'S NAMES

The ability to remember people's names and to use them is an important skill in every profession where people's support is essential. One American newspaper considers it so important to get people's names right that the journalists lose a day's pay for spelling a name incorrectly.

A student on one of my courses wrote to me:

> "When I read through the section of your course notes on remembering people's names, it reminded me of a most important lesson I was to learn when starting out in my career! During my second month of college, our professor gave us a quiz. I was a conscientious student and had breezed through the questions, until I read the last one: 'What is the first name of the woman who cleans the school?'
>
> Surely this was some kind of joke. I had seen the cleaning woman several times. She was tall, dark-haired and in her 50s, but how would I know her name? I handed in my paper, leaving the last question blank. Before class ended, I asked if the last question would count toward our quiz grade. 'Absolutely,' said the professor. 'In your careers you will meet many people. All are significant. They deserve your attention and care, even if all you do is smile and say "hello".' I've never forgotten that lesson. I also learned her name was Dorothy."

If you have problems remembering names, you may find the following helpful:

- When being introduced to someone, make sure you hear their name properly.
- Do not be embarrassed about asking someone to repeat or spell their name. Most people will be pleased you were interested enough to ask.
- Use the person's name as often as is appropriate during the discussion.

- Repeat the name to yourself during the conversation.
- On parting, use the name again.
- Most important of all, having met new acquaintances, mentally review their names when you get a quiet moment.
- Practise remembering the names of people who work with your customer, such as receptionists and secretaries.

Remember that there is no such thing as a bad memory, just an untrained one. It is possible in a short time to improve your retention dramatically by applying these basic memory skills.

Some people can take names to the extreme by overusing them in conversation. Also, memorising names for the purpose of trying to create an impression is certainly viewed by many as just another sales technique, so try to find a happy medium.

Develop Positive People Skills

One thing is certain, if you choose to manage salespeople, you will need to appraise yourself constantly on people skills.

- Be conscious of the difference between a punishment and a correction. A punishment is given in public with the intention of humiliating. A correction is given in private with calmness and sincerity and with the intention of helping the offender.
- If you must knock somebody else's idea, do it gently, never maliciously and only when you can come up with a better one yourself.
- Try to create an atmosphere in which others never feel threatened or manipulated.
- Never miss an opportunity to say something positive to others on their achievement, no matter how small or insignificant it may appear.
- Avoid being a John Blunt, the painter of the worst picture.

- Never back down from a commitment; promises made should be kept, regardless of cost or personal embarrassment.
- Make a point of being tolerant. It's nice to be important but more important to be nice.
- Bring others into the "team" by asking their advice and opinions.
- Be upright and honest in your dealings. Let others know that they are dealing with someone they can trust.
- Develop a reputation for being fair and just in your appraisal of others.
- Show by example and never expect others to do what you wouldn't do yourself.
- Avoid comparing people with others and don't expect anybody to imitate the ideals of another.
- Be a comfortable person to be with and cultivate the quality of being stimulating and interesting.
- Learn and use the names of supposedly unimportant people.
- Compliment and encourage often, but avoid flattery at all costs.

If you have inherited a few washed-out salespeople, it can be difficult to sustain their long-term motivation — you need to dispense with ideas that clearly won't work. The carrot of financial rewards may have little effect if their families have already grown up and motivation through fear of losing their jobs will have the opposite effect. Work harder at finding things about them that you like, make them feel as if they are important members of your team, communicate friend-to-friend, be encouraging and watch them go.

PERSONAL ACTIVITY

Take a sheet of paper and draw a line down the centre from top to bottom. On the left-hand side write down all of the positive qualities that you admire in others, things that people do or say that motivate and inspire you to positive action. On the right-hand side write down all the de-motivating traits or personality aspects that you find offensive or unacceptable in other people. Take a highlighter and endorse all the positive and negative traits that you sincerely believe you possess. Make a positive decision to work on eliminating all the negatives. If you find these traits offensive, there is a real chance that others will also. Work with determination to develop new skills and accentuate the positives that you already possess.

Take another sheet of paper and select somebody who plays a special part in your life. Take as much time as you require writing down all of the special qualities that you believe that person possesses. Complete this exercise before you read any further.

Hopefully you have come up with a good number of points and the purpose of the exercise is this: How would they react if they knew how you felt about them? How much motivation would you get by telling them? When are you going to tell them?

Finally, do whatever it is that is necessary to establish and maintain an ever-friendly atmosphere within the company. If staff don't get on, rectify it; if a manager's attitude is wrong, correct it; if people you pay to give support do not support you, find out what is causing the problem and work out a solution.

Ten Key Points from Creating and Sustaining a Positive Working Environment

1. Early morning attitudes set the tone for the rest of the working day. If you cannot be in good humour in the morning, at least avoid being in a bad one.
2. Check what you think and check what you say. If you think negatively, you will communicate in a negative manner.
3. Avoid depressing conversation like the plague: bad weather, an increase in mortgage rates or the gory details of nature's latest catastrophe will do little for morale or motivation. However, when confronted with genuine bad news from your salespeople, deal with it immediately and approach it in a positive way.
4. Invest in motivating self-development material that your salespeople can listen to in the car. If background music is a must — ensure that it is stimulating and cheerful.
5. Create and maintain an attitude of customer-mindedness with all support staff.
6. Admit your mistakes, ask salespeople for opinions and never miss an opportunity to say "well done".
7. Everybody associated with the business creates your organisation's profile in the industry. Encourage your people to build and maintain a climate of outstanding professionalism in all aspects of their job, their appearance and everything they do.
8. Bring others into the team by asking their advice and opinions.
9. Learn to use people's names, but avoid overdoing it.
10. Have a look at your company from the outside; what impressions are created? The litter outside your office may not be yours but its existence does nothing for your corporate image.

Chapter Five

Recruiting and Keeping Top Salespeople

Any company sincere about reducing the turnover of its people must look at all the elements that affect morale, attitude and motivation of the sales force. Therein lies the key to retaining or losing good people. Too many companies think in terms of recruiting costs while blindly ignoring the consequential cost of losing top people.

When a salesperson hands in their month's notice, their motivation to achieve results in their last four weeks is diminished. From notice to quit to actual termination, the manager can anticipate a downturn in sales. Add to this the impact of the departure on other salespeople's motivation and the hidden losses lurking in customer reaction. The public relations aspects can't be overlooked if there is abnormal frequency in the change of sales personnel.

Apart from the disruptive elements, consider the time-consuming management effort involved in interviewing, recruiting and developing a new salesperson to the same level of the previous employee. Monetary costs accrue, such as payments to agencies and setting up new employee records, but what is the real cost of losing a top salesperson? Whatever the expenditure, it is not worth it if the departure is the result of less than diligent management.

Recruitment — The Usual Sources

As a preliminary stage in recruiting staff, a thoroughly analytical approach must involve scrutiny of the sources from which the candidates will be coming. If you are investing heavily in costly newspaper design and using the advertisement as prestige projection for the company, your marketing department will be evaluating the response and no doubt, your financial director will be evaluating the cost.

Managers can seek recruits through employment agencies, which are generally adequate, but this depends on the agency, and experience of using them will prove to be your best guide. However, head-hunting tends to be the most effective method, especially when time and cost are taken into consideration.

However, before you invest in advertising or recruiting agencies, be sure to look at resources from within. It is always good for company morale to look at existing employees and consider their chances of making the grade. Of course, if an existing employee makes the shortlist and is being weighed in the balance, the temptation can be to go for the devil you know rather than the one you don't. Experience indicates that we should adhere to the job description and give it to the best candidate.

GETTING IT RIGHT — AT THE START

Staff turnover can be reduced before it is allowed to happen — at the selection interview. This is usually a moment of high drama, for both the prospective candidate and the employer.

When companies advertise for their "ideal" salesperson, they soon realise this person doesn't exist and then compromise on their requirements. Where this compromise stops is a key issue. Not only does the company have to consider whether this is the right person for the company, but also whether this is the right company for the salesperson.

Employing good people is an expensive job but it is never as costly as employing the wrong ones. This will usually happen for two major reasons: either the company or the salesperson don't live up to expectations. It is important, therefore, to ensure that the needs of both parties are met. The final selection is the crucial area for that decision.

At the recruiting stage, much emphasis is placed on the company's requirements but little, if any, on the expectations of the individual salesperson. It is useful for the interviewer to build the following questions into the interview:

- How does this job fit into your own personal plans for the future?
- What precisely do you expect from this company or your immediate manager?
- What elements of the overall compensation package, if any, concern you and why?

Anything other than an appropriate positive response is a danger signal to employing the prospective candidate. A salesperson coming into a company where there is a "real" or "perceived" inequity will be starting with a severe disadvantage that will lead to motivational problems down the line.

Several years ago as a sales manager with a multinational, I was anxious to ensure that the people I had selected would not be exposed to circumstances that were not covered at the interview. I realised I was giving the prospective salespeople my "personal view" about our wonderful company, but this view was not necessarily shared by the salespeople reporting to me. I was prepared to state truthfully how good it was and reveal how bad it could be. I decided to offer the three selected candidates the opportunity to interview our salespeople. They all felt this was a chance not to be missed.

I selected three sales personnel for the interview, the most experienced, the least experienced and one person who was going through a bad patch. I instructed them to answer all questions truthfully and to give as much information as requested. On completion of the interviews, each of the candidates announced they wanted the job . . . each one was employed.

This policy proved to be so successful in all future recruiting that in the succeeding five years we never had one single case of a salesperson complaining about being misled, let down or made promises which were not honoured.

An important aspect of this process was giving each of the candidates an individually guided tour of the offices and in particular their prospective slot. I was anxious that the working environment would not compare unfavourably with their current situation. Perhaps it has crossed your mind that the reason this policy was introduced was because we had plenty to offer in terms of perks, pleasant working conditions and a highly successful track record as an employer. On the contrary: the situation was the complete reverse.

Tips on Interviewing Salespeople

Remember that interviewing is a two-way process. If any one of the parties feels "let down", it is unlikely the relationship will be permanent. For that reason, it is important that both parties know exactly what is expected of each other.

Be conscious of "overselling" the job. Too many interviewers tell the applicant only the positive elements of the position without ever addressing the downside. For example, a former candidate told me he was looking for a new job after only 12 months with the company. When I enquired what had happened, he replied:

> "At the interview, I was given the impression within six months I could expect to be moving to a more senior position. While I was not specifically promised promotion it was implied that I would get the job if it became available — it did become available and I didn't get it."

Allowing salespeople to leave an interview with an unjustified high level of expectation will not only put considerable pressure on the manager to deliver, but it will also cause serious motivational problems if things do not go according to plan. This serious issue can be avoided by telling the applicant:

- What is expected of him or her, the rewards for achieving targets and the long-term possibilities. This information should be factual and based on all the evidence available from actual performance of the sales team.

- How bad the job can be, the traveling involved, the paperwork, the difficult customers, the irritating policy quirks and so on. Can he or she handle this?
- What happens if he or she does not achieve targets? How quickly do the company expect results? What kind of support can the salesperson expect?

The advantage of being totally honest with the salesperson is reflected in the knowledge that one of the biggest singular reasons for the job turnover of salespeople is they feel "let down" or "commitments made at the time of the interview never materialised". Telling it like it is eliminates this problem.

Prepare properly for each interview. Avoid yes or no responses to questions and probe for in-depth answers. The purpose of the interview is to employ the best people available. John Fenton, in his book *How to Double your Profits within a Year* (Pan), claims that there are four principal faults committed by interviewers:

a) Failure to prepare properly;

b) Failure to banish any interruptions while the interview is proceeding;

c) Failure to relax the interviewee and get him or her talking freely;

d) Failure to ask direct, probing and sometimes blunt questions.

Interviewing time is expensive, so avoid too much small talk. In some cases, it will be obvious the person applying is not suitable for the position. Get into the habit of telling each applicant the interview will be brief so as not to offend. This allows you to give extra time to more suitable applicants. Inform the applicant the interview is strictly confidential and no references will be taken up without his or her permission. The job will be subject to the provision of satisfactory references. If you find contradictions in the answers, probe to find the reasons and avoid prejudging the applicant; wait until all the facts are elicited before making a decision.

Danger Signals to Watch out for when Recruiting Salespeople

Interviewers are human beings with feelings and emotions. As a result, their objectivity can be swayed by personal feelings towards the interviewees. We may like the person and want to employ them because they "fit in" with the rest of the team. To assist in maintaining a view free of emotion or bias towards or against the candidate, the following are some of the danger signals, which indicate caution is advisable:

Frequent change of jobs?

What were the reasons given? An unstable career background is an obvious "red flag" area. Unless plausible reasons are submitted for frequent change, the interviewee is likely to continue "job hopping".

"Breaks" in employment?

Breaks such as finishing one job in September and starting again in November. As a rule, most successful people move directly from one job into another. A salesperson who claims he left to "better himself" would not better himself by becoming unemployed, unless he can prove to you that he did so for very positive reasons, such as further full-time education. It may be an educational experience to phone the company that employed him up to the time of the "break".

Domestic circumstances?

Probing into people's personal lives is an extremely sensitive issue and for any other job, questions of this nature would be considered an invasion of privacy. In fact, in some countries it is now an offence to ask people about their personal circumstances and while this "privacy law" is understandable it doesn't make interviewing any easier. Selling is a difficult job and the last thing we need is a salesperson whose family circumstances is an added handicap. Because of the nature of the job you need to find out how he or she would feel about:

- Staying away overnight
- Being away for periods of time
- Attending training or meetings at night or weekends
- Working under pressure of achieving results
- Entertaining customers

The time to make a decision about whether to accept an individual's personal circumstances is at the interviewing stage, not two or three months into their employment. I have also employed excellent people only to discover that his or her partner doesn't like being left alone, that one of their children attends a special school and therefore cannot start before 9.30, or some ailing relative needs to attend a clinic every Thursday. If I had this information at the time of the interview, I may still have employed them but I would certainly have negotiated a different contract.

There is a dilemma here, as you generally cannot ask about these things explicitly. However, if the interviewee is happy to volunteer the information, you do not have to worry about accusations of discrimination. The best solution is, of course, a win-win one: if you describe to the potential salesperson the type of flexibility and benefits your company is willing to provide, they will usually respond in kind by telling you any special needs they may have. You can then work together on a mutually beneficial contract, including a certain amount of "give and take".

Outside interests?

Talking about other interests is a good way to get an interviewee to "open up". However, is there any reason to think "unacceptable working time" will be devoted to these interests? All managers recognise that their staff will occasionally do some personal "errands" during office hours and, provided the freedom is not abused, there is rarely any difficulty. However, employing somebody who has the motivation to do other things during business hours may be a different matter.

Is there a tendency to blame others?

Is the candidate hypercritical of former employers, colleagues or managers? Avoid whiners like the plague! Is there evidence of exaggerated sales achievements to unrealistic levels? While personal confidence is a necessary quality in selling, a deliberate attempt to deceive is a clear indication the person is anything but confident. Beware of those who are "legends in their own mind". The common denominator of top salespeople is they never "blow" excessively — even at interviews.

Job research?

If the interviewee has little knowledge of your company, it probably means he or she is only looking for a job and not a career. For somebody coming straight from college, this point might be overlooked at the first interview, but not for an experienced salesperson.

Lack of knowledge of the company products, especially by an experienced sales applicant, is a danger signal. Top salespeople want to work for companies whose products sell. If he or she didn't take time to check out the product, it is fair to assume there may be "other reasons" for leaving the present job and they should be investigated thoroughly. My firm conclusion is that if the interviewees don't take the time to inform themselves of fundamental factors, they should be automatically precluded. I may have missed one or two good people because of this policy, but one thing is certain: a lot of unsuitable candidates hit the dust.

What do the references say?

What is not said is important. Most companies feel an obligation to provide staff with a reference on termination of employment — particularly when one is requested by the staff member. To refuse may cause all sorts of unnecessary headaches. A cleverly worded reference is all that is required to satisfy the recipient. For example, if the person had been dismissed for poor sales, the letter of recommendation will have no reference to selling ability. If the characteristics you desire are not mentioned, beware. All references should be checked out with a telephone call and a most searching question is: "Would you re-employ this individual?"

Prepared to accept a similar package?

Let's be totally realistic about this: few salespeople are prepared to move for the same package that they are currently receiving. It is certainly advisable to be suspect about the real motivation for their desire to change jobs.

Are all past employers given as referees?

If not, why not? A personality clash or a bad decision by the interviewee is quite acceptable but if an applicant has not given a former employer as a referee it may spell danger. Ask the interviewee why they have not given the specific company for reference purposes.

How does the applicant score on social skills?

Unlike any other profession, salespeople are required to score highly in terms of the social graces and the absence of these talents at the interview is a cause for concern. Look out for:

- A defensive manner
- No enthusiasm

- Poor appearance
- Lack of confidence
- No questions to ask.

Other areas that might spell danger are:

- No thought put into personal goals
- Solely interested in money
- Poorly prepared CV
- Arriving late for the interview
- Casual approach.

It is fair to assume that the interviewees are giving their best at this important meeting. If their "best" is suspect, a decision not to employ them is a wise one! As a further guideline, the following criteria merit serious consideration:

- *Physical make-up*: Would a customer be offended in any way, for example, by the individual's personal hygiene?
- *Attainments*: What level of education or skill must the person have as minimum standard?
- *General intelligence*: Able to work without supervision?
- *Special aptitudes*: Does the person have any additional aptitudes that would be of benefit to you?
- *Disposition*: Able to get along with others? Conscientious? Reliable? Punctual? Introverted?
- *Motivation*: Do he or she really want this job and why?
- *Desire*: Has he or she convinced you that they are motivated to achieve success in your business.
- *Attitude*: Is the attitude positive or negative?

Questions Asked by Interviewers

Listed here are ten questions that could be asked at an interview. It is unlikely that all questions would be asked at the same meeting but by carefully selecting the questions, one should have a reasonably comprehensive profile of the candidate.

- What do you like most about your current job?
- What do you feel you accomplished in your career to date?
- How would you describe yourself?
- Where do you see yourself in five years' time?
- How do you feel about making presentations to large groups?
- How do you get on with people?
- How do you feel about working under pressure?
- What interests you most about this particular position?
- What are you looking for in a job?
- What kind of decisions do you have difficulty making?

Remember, interviewing is not a battle of wits, it should be an occasion where the interviewee is made to feel comfortable, relaxed and encouraged to give the best account of themselves. Be considerate to people who are tense or nervous; it may well be that they are "all wound up" about the prospects of working with you.

Reducing Turnover of Salespeople

From personal knowledge and reports, identify all the possible causes for job leaving. Remember, you are concerned only with controllable causes. You can't find a solution to a problem if you can't identify what the problem is.

- When you hear people complaining, listen carefully or you might miss valuable information.

- What are the facts and circumstances of your last departure from the company?
- What percentage of people leave every year?
- Do your people enjoy their work?
- Is there a problem with a supervisor or manager?
- Do your rivals do it differently or better?

Eliminate the causes

Having analysed reasons for leaving, if the same reason is repeated, you have identified one serious problem area. If this is not eliminated, there will be further departures. Remember, avoidable loss of one good person is one too many.

Talk to your sales team

One sure way of reducing staff turnover is to talk with your sales team and give them periodic opportunities to get things "off their chest". The benefits are enormous. It cannot be overemphasised that, for the following ideas to work, it is important that the manager conducts the exercise out of sincere interest and not as a management technique.

If there is ever the slightest suggestion that people will be reprimanded or penalised for holding unpopular views, they will tell you only what they believe you want to hear and the entire exercise will be wasted.

Demonstrate by your body language, facial expression and manner that their comments, regardless of how much you may want to "jump in" and disagree, are of real interest to you. Your role is only to listen and not to judge. If anybody feels threatened by your reactions they will withdraw from the discussion. Here are some of the benefits of listening to what salespeople have to say:

- Salespeople appreciate being allowed to speak their minds because by doing so they feel their opinions are helping to influence events and policy. It allows them to feel "in on things".

- The manager has so much to learn about his or her management style by allowing staff to make observations as to how it can be improved. Remember, the best learning experience for a sales manager is an uninhibited salesperson. Not listening to his or her views is comparable to a salesperson not listening to the views of the customer.
- No two people are the same! Allowing people to express their discontent with company policy or a turn of events may identify valuable individual needs.
- Frank and open discussion devoid of anger and tension is a win-win situation. There are no losers — provided the comments are listened to sincerely and acted upon.

Carry out periodic work reviews

Salespeople like to know where they stand, how they are doing, what needs to be improved and where they are going. Discussions conducted in a tension-free environment obviate a great deal of turmoil. Ideally, the review should be carried out every three months and should not just be used to tell salespeople where they stand but also to allow them to tell you where you stand.

Lee Iacocca, the Chrysler chairman, according to his biography, favours quarterly reviews. He finds the increased interaction is healthy and keeps the good people from getting lost in the system while preventing the cowboys from hiding.

A skill I used with my sales supervisors was to fill in a work review on many of the behavioural aspects of their job, such as their constant level of motivation, and their attitudes towards their job, the company, their staff and me as their manager. When I had completed their reviews, I took out a blank review sheet and asked them to do one on me. While most of them were reluctant to be overly critical of my management style, there was sufficient information "between the lines" for me to learn where I could improve in my attitudes towards them. It was a positive exercise and it sent a message to each of them that their manager was not above learning.

The exit interview

So much useful information can be gleaned from this approach to salespeople who have decided to leave. Once the individual is convinced you are sincere in your attempts to find the reason for their departure, they may decide to tell you why. It is not always a good idea for the salesperson's immediate manager to conduct the exit interview — particularly if he or she is one of the reasons for departure.

The post-exit interview

If possible, contact former employees who may have a useful contribution to make to your records. After a time-span of several months, former employees can usually give a fair and accurate appraisal of why circumstances dictated that their future lay elsewhere.

There is another interesting aspect to contacting former employees; you may discover they have made a mistake in moving to their new company. They may be only too anxious to discuss the possibility of returning.

Ten Key Points from Recruiting and Keeping Top Salespeople

1. Staff turnover can be reduced before it is ever allowed to happen — at the selection interview.
2. Whatever it costs you to get the right people, it can never be as costly as employing the wrong ones!
3. Try and find a balance between what you are looking for in a salesperson and what the salesperson's expectations are in the job. Failure to do so causes problems down the line!

4. Interviewing is a two-way process. Ensure that the position you are offering does not compare unfavourably with the salesperson's present job, otherwise he or she is starting at a disadvantage.
5. Watch out for danger signals such as breaks in employment and frequent change of jobs or failure to find out about your company.
6. It is fair to assume that prospective new recruits are giving their best at the selection interview — if their best is not good enough, don't employ them!
7. Identify all the reasons why salespeople have left you in the past and work with diligence to eliminate controllable causes!
8. One way to reduce staff turnover is to give salespeople ample opportunity to get things off their chest. Be sure to listen or you might lose another!
9. Carry out periodic work reviews. This prevents a situation where good people get lost in the system and ensures that the poor performers have no place to hide!
10. Give your salespeople occasional opportunities to do an assessment on you and your management style.

Chapter Six

Contracts of Employment

This chapter concentrates on the essential procedures that must also be put in place if all your hard-earned motivation is to be maintained — permanently.

This chapter has three main objectives:

- Assuming that you found the right people, to provide you with an *agreed* contract of employment, which states in very clear terms exactly what is expected of both parties.
- To act as a permanent reminder to management that in order for the contract to work, they *must* honour their side of the bargain.
- To offer guidance on what needs to be done to maintain the enormous goodwill that should result from the implementation of such a positive document.

The immediate, short- and long-term motivation of your team is greatly influenced by the presence or absence of an *agreed* contract of employment. Handing staff a document outlining the various ways in which they can be disciplined or dismissed may protect management but it does nothing to establish or maintain harmonious relationships.

How you design or implement a "contract" is a matter of personal choice. Trying to strike a balance between designing a motivating win-win document while also providing maximum protection for both parties requires a lot of imagination — but it can be done!

Why are Contracts of Employment Important?

Many large organisations already have contracts and the sales manager may not be allowed to create another, but that should not prevent you from having a written understanding of the relationship and the requirements for the job. Thus each "understanding" could be personalised for each individual.

There are many unassailable reasons why managers should have a contract of employment and not only for salespeople but also for every member of staff. If introduced in a positive spirit, what it will do is:

- Improve and maintain staff motivation;
- Reduce the frequency of discipline meetings;
- Keep every member of the team focused on individual job objectives;
- Help to maintain better management/staff relations;
- Act as a permanent reminder to staff of the importance of what management perceives to be the key issues;
- Assist management in achieving business goals.

Apart from the motivational aspects of the contract there are other more serious reasons why the implementation of contracts should move up the list of priorities:

- Depending on your own country's legislation, you may be legally *obliged* to provide each member of staff with a contract of employment.
- In the event of a member of staff having to be disciplined, suspended or dismissed, the contract *may* become a crucial document.
- If a "dismissed" employee decides to take action against you, the contract *will definitely* become a crucial document.

You do not have to be an expert in labour law to understand the fundamentals and it is strongly recommended that, in tandem with the design of a contract of employment, you read all of the relevant labour legislation. If that is not possible, ensure that legal advice is sought on the content of the contract before you introduce it to staff.

INTRODUCING CONTRACTS OF EMPLOYMENT

Management attitude to the introduction of the contract is absolutely crucial. If your motivation for introducing contracts is purely self-protection, it simply will not work. On the other hand, a manager implementing a contract for the most positive reasons may still have to win over people who are understandably sceptical of written agreements. A few suggestions on how you might introduce contracts are as follows:

- At your next sales meeting, explain that you wish to bring about the introduction of win-win contracts of employment and you see this prospective document as an opportunity for management and staff to enter into the spirit of a new and rewarding relationship.
- Explain that you would like the details of the contract to be *agreed*, rather than management acting independently, or imposing their views on staff.
- Explain also that when new people join the company, you would like to be able to claim that the "contract" accurately reflects the spirit that prevails between management and staff.
- Give each staff member a copy of the "draft" contract and provide an explanation as to why some points were considered important enough to include.
- It is essential that staff also understand clearly that this document is not a one-way process. Demonstrate your goodwill by outlining the positive changes you are prepared to make to bring about new management attitudes.

- Allow them to take away the draft contract to discuss it amongst themselves. Show willingness to *consider* any reasonable argument to add, subtract or delete any paragraph or wording that they may deem to be unreasonable.

Comfort yourself in the knowledge that on any occasion where contracts have been introduced in the manner outlined above, salespeople have responded enthusiastically and without any suggested changes. It is also important to note that as much of the content of the contract relates to mutual obligations under the law, there are not that many changes that a staff member can recommend.

Writing up the Details of the Contract

Failure to have a written *mutually agreed* understanding of the working relationship puts management at a major disadvantage and a contract *mutually endorsed by both parties* can help to establish a positive foundation on which new relationships can be built.

You may not like the "sample" contract as outlined later in this chapter and clearly it is an extensive document. It is your privilege to include aspects appropriate to your business and to subtract or delete any references or paragraphs. However before you try to get it to fit on two pages, remember that it will only take a salesperson five minutes to read and it can save everybody a lot of grief later on.

Introducing the Contract to the New Employee

First impressions are lasting impressions and the spirit in which the document is written obviously influences reader perception. This should outline and provide:

- A warm friendly welcome to the business;
- An explanation that the purpose of the contract is to protect both parties;

- An expression of the wish that the relationship will be long term;
- An invitation to the reader to question and query the details before signing.

If the introduction is written in a warm, friendly and inviting manner (as of course it should be), the reader is likely to take a more balanced view of the need for "rules" which, inevitably, they will read later.

Management Philosophy

There is little point in having positive business goals if the people who are expected to assist in achieving them don't know what the goals are. As a special exercise, select members of staff and management at random and ask them to outline the aims of the business. While the bottom line may be to make a profit, asking staff how they intend to bring this about may provide some interesting answers. For example, a manager who thinks that the *priority* of his or her job is to keep staff on their toes may think this leads to greater profitability; in reality it may create the very opposite. Writing down the goals doesn't guarantee their achievement but it will certainly help.

What Salespeople Can Expect from Management

It is strongly recommended that you think carefully through any promises you intend to make to staff because you will be expected to honour them to the letter.

There is absolutely nothing written in this sample contract that should cause management even the slightest discomfort. Outside of what you are legally obliged to provide, your only commitment is to have regular meetings with your staff and to be reasonable in your attitude — the absence of which will in any circumstances cause serious motivational problems. On closer examination, you will note that you are only providing the basic minimum that staff can reasonably expect from management.

What Management Expect from Salespeople

Outlining clearly what needs to be done can dilute much management and staff frustration. *Telling* an individual will never be as powerful as providing an explanation in black and white. Furthermore, as staff should only be assessed against what they know to be their job, it is essential to have agreed documented evidence of what that job involves!

Dress Code

Fortunately, the standards of salespeople's appearance right across the spectrum of industry tend to be extremely high. There are exceptions, of course, and this is where dress code needs to be enshrined in a document that salespeople are expected to sign.

The introduction of a contract creates a significant opportunity for management to state, in unambiguous terms, the absolute minimum standards acceptable for people working in the industry. Some companies insist on business suits while others, such as banks, have a uniform. Where do you draw the line on appearance and how can salespeople be expected to maintain a standard if they don't know what that standard is?

A few years ago, I carried out training for a builders' providers and part of my brief was to assist management in improving the image of individuals within the sales force. Two of the salespeople had the entrenched view that if you were selling to a builder it would be helpful if you dressed like one yourself. One of the salespeople would not be convinced otherwise and further discussion culminated in his dismissal. He subsequently took an action against the company and won his case. It was adjudged to be unfair to dismiss on the basis of appearance, if a standard of "personal appearance" was not included in the job specification.

Having a statement about this sensitive issue, or others such as smoking, endorsed in a contract may not eliminate the problem, but it will give you the right to insist that they do something about it!

Recording Information

Even if you possess a super-power memory, you will be hard-pressed to remember the salient details of every important transaction or conversation. However, I am more concerned here with the use of a diary insofar as it fits into the overall concept of the contract.

A manager should never keep a diary solely for cynical reasons. However, in the event of a staff member not working out, a diary may become a useful document. Lateness or absence from work, and in particular verbal warnings, must be recorded as part of a potential discipline process.

Hopefully you will never need to refer to this information but if you do, times, dates and what was said and in whose presence may subsequently become important. Managers are expected to act reasonably and in accordance with strict procedures; therefore it will be helpful in demonstrating and supplying proof that certain guidelines were followed.

Updating Contracts

Because the law is ever-changing, management should insist that salespeople be kept informed regularly of changes that affect them and the customer. One way to do this is to provide each member of staff with a binder that they should update regularly and the contract could be the first document that goes into this folder.

One important benefit of having contracts is that the details can be fine-tuned to apply to all levels of staff and management. Also, as labour legislation is an ongoing process, it will always be easier to add information to a document than it will ever be to create one from scratch.

SAMPLE CONTRACT OF EMPLOYMENT

Employee: ____________________

Address: ____________________

____

Start Date ____________________

Job Title ____________________

Tel No: ____________________

Employer: ____________________

Address ____________________

____

Contents

- *Introduction and Welcome*
- *Management Philosophy*
- *What You Can Expect From Us*
- *What We Can Expect From You*
- *Assessment Period*
- *Job Description*
- *Dress Code*
- *Working Hours*
- *Expenses & Entertaining*
- *Care of Company Transport*
- *Selling Equipment*
- *Salary Reviews*
- *Payment Arrangements*
- *Holidays*
- *Sickness and Absence*
- *Sales Performance Reviews and Assessments*

- *Payroll/Holiday/Absence*
- *Code of Conduct*

Introduction

First of all, I want to extend a special welcome to you from the management and staff. I trust that this will be the start of a long and happy association and the experience gained in working with the rest of the team will be fulfilling, rewarding and enjoyable.

For people with the right attitude, prepared to put in the effort and learn about this profession, the opportunities are exciting and never more so than they are now! We are committed to providing you with training and development that is appropriate to your job, and this, combined with your continuing experience, can only enhance your prospects of a rewarding career in this industry.

My purpose in presenting you with this document before you start is to ensure that, as far as is possible, both of us have a clear understanding of what is expected of each other. It is not just a series of management guidelines; it is also essential that people entering our business have a reasonable appreciation of the ever-increasing special demands made of people in our profession.

Some of the language used is quite formal, but please understand that in some cases we felt it was useful to quote the actual wording of the legislation. As an employee, you also have rights and I have included your entitlements as laid down under the appropriate labour laws. We will both hope that disciplinary measures will never be required, but once again, it is important to understand the procedures we must follow in the unlikely event of any action being calling for.

Outside of our mutual obligations, we must always remember that we exist in the most competitive of all markets and our customers have a choice! A lack of care, interest or enthusiasm can cause us countless problems and unhappy customers may decide never to deal with us again. It will be a combination of patience, courtesy and a desire to provide outstanding service, which will separate us from all our competitors, provide long-term security for our business and create greater opportunities for our staff.

Once again, welcome and good luck!

P.S. If any of the points require further explanation, please bring it to my attention.

Management Philosophy

It is obviously important that you have a clear understanding of the aims of our business and we hope you will play an enthusiastic part in helping us achieve our goals.

- *We want to be regarded as the best company within our market area.*
- *We shall endeavour, at all times, to provide outstanding proactive service to our customers.*
- *Regardless of the level of purchase or customer manner, we will provide equally high standards of service.*
- *Every person that phones, calls or writes or visits our premises will be treated with outstanding courtesy.*
- *Every customer who receives a call from our sales team will be treated with the utmost courtesy and the highest standards of professional selling.*
- *We will all play our part in maintaining friendly relations and outstanding teamwork at all levels of the company.*

It may not be possible to achieve our objectives on every occasion, but a team committed to a common goal of achieving total customer satisfaction will benefit everybody.

What You Can Expect from Management

Your continuous motivation to carry out your job with enthusiasm is of prime importance to the achievement of our stated objectives. Therefore, management will and must provide you with the support and encouragement necessary to fulfil your function. Our commitment to you is:

- *That you will receive adequate training for any role you are asked to undertake.*
- *We will explain, whenever necessary, why something should be done.*
- *We will make special efforts to be reasonable in attitude at all times.*
- *We will not only listen to, but also welcome your suggestions.*
- *We will make it a point of expressing appreciation for a job well done.*
- *We will review your progress regularly and encourage your further development.*
- *We will, at all times, be empathetic when assessing your performance.*

Managers are also capable of making mistakes and, with the best of intentions, matters important to staff can sometimes be overlooked. In the event of a management oversight, it is hoped that you will bring the matter to our attention.

What We Expect From You

Our purpose in employing you is that you will make a positive contribution to our overall efforts and play your part in maintaining excellent teamwork and high customer service standards. We ask that you:

- *Will work as a positive member of the team.*

- *Greet our customers in a friendly and courteous manner at all times.*
- *Endorse our selling philosophy and practise our selling methods.*
- *Be considerate to fellow employees.*
- *Be ever-courteous to colleagues, managers and customers.*
- *Give outstanding service to customers.*
- *Go about your job in an enthusiastic manner.*
- *Keep personal or domestic problems outside of work.*
- *Strive continually to improve our standards.*
- *Follow training guidelines and attend all sales development programmes.*

There is also an attitudinal side of the job, which can be difficult to measure, and this requires that you provide a service to all our customers in a manner that indicates patience and courtesy. Inevitably, we will get some things wrong, but each complaint is an opportunity to show our professionalism and demonstrate that we do actually want the customer's business.

Assessment Period

We are offering you this job because we believe you demonstrate the attributes necessary to carry out the role with competence and enthusiasm. An assessment period of six months will apply from the date of commencement of employment. During this period, management will have regular meetings with you to appraise your performance on the basis of:

- *Overall job performance and competence in carrying out your tasks;*
- *Your potential to achieve sales targets;*
- *Your willingness to do your job and your attitude to customers, colleagues and management;*

- *Personal standards such as time keeping and appearance.*

On the basis of these assessments, management will extend the assessment period, continue with or terminate your employment. It is also hoped that you will use this period to evaluate the management against your expectations. Offering you a permanent position is only part of the consideration — we accept that you must also be happy to stay with us.

Job Description

Your Job Title is: Major Account Executive
You will be directly responsible to: [Name and Title]
You will be engaged in one or a combination of the following duties:

- *Completing all sales administration;*
- *Presenting sales projections;*
- *Canvassing for new business;*
- *Calling on established customers;*
- *Drawing up sales proposals;*
- *Achieving agreed sales targets;*
- *Carrying out post-sales courtesy calls;*
- *Any other duties in line with the achievement of targets.*

You will be required to be flexible and willing to undertake any task applicable to the running of our business. Such duties may be outside the area of your normal duties.

The standard of service that we as a team provide to our customers can significantly boost our sales and profits or threaten our very survival. It can take years of positive teamwork to inspire somebody to become a customer but it only takes one staff member a few seconds to lose one.

Place of Work

Your normal place of work is at this location: [Address]
[NB — If you have more than one branch, and the employee is required to work between these outlets, you should insert the following clause:]

You will normally/mainly [delete as appropriate] *be required to work at the company/firm's premises at* [address] *but you may be required, from time to time, to work at the premises of such subsidiary companies or organisations as the company/firm may require. You will be given as much notice of any such change as is reasonably practicable.*

Dress Code

You are expected to present yourself to our customers in a professional manner and that includes a high standard of personal presentation at all times. [If your people are dealing with food or other sensitive materials you may wish to include very specific guidelines.]

Working Hours

We start at 8.30 a.m. and the office closes at 5.30. Because of the nature of your job, you will be expected to make yourself available after hours for training, sales meetings and occasionally calling on customers not available any earlier.

Expenses and Entertaining

Expenses are paid on the first Friday of every month. These expenses must be receipted and signed off by a manager and will only include: [Explain what is covered].

Care of company transport

You will be provided with [make of car], *which will remain the property of the company, and it is entirely your responsibility to ensure that it is serviced regularly and kept clean and in good repair at all times.*

Selling equipment

You will be supplied with laptop, briefcase and sales presentation materials and it is requested that you care for them in a manner consistent with your role as a professional salesperson. We want to be perceived as a high quality company; therefore everything we present to our customers must be in the area of professional excellence.

Salary reviews

Wage reviews normally take place in line with national wage agreements and are implemented from [put in the date]. *Unless otherwise stated at commencement of employment, the first review will be on completion of one year's service.*

Payment arrangements

You will be paid monthly by cash/cheque/direct debit on the [day] *of each month.* [Explain any other details such as deductions or bonus payments and how they will be calculated.]

Holidays

The Company's holiday year runs from ______ to ______ .

The holiday entitlement for the leave year is [number of] *days.*

When a termination of this contract occurs and the paid holidays already taken exceed the paid holiday entitlement on the date of termination, the company will deduct the excess holiday pay from any termination pay.

No more than ____ working days can be taken together at any one time.

Requests for annual leave must be made to management at least two weeks in advance.

Sickness/Absenteeism

In the event of absence from work, you are requested to contact management within one hour of starting time on the first day of absence. A medical certificate is required for illness lasting in excess of two days and on a weekly basis thereafter. The company/firm reserves the right to make its own judgment on the justification for any absence.

[If there are any circumstances in which an employee will not be paid, that should also be explained here.]

Sales Performance Review and Assessments

You are being offered this position on the understanding that you are the best candidate to fulfil this role and you will be measured on the basis of the consistent achievement of agreed sales objectives.

These reviews will take place every three months and you will be given notice as to when to attend. At this assessment, we will review the following:

- *Achievement of sales against agreed objectives;*
- *Your ongoing training and development;*
- *Projections for the rest of the selling campaign;*
- *Back-up and support required;*
- *A plan of action to be reviewed at the next three month assessment.*

You will also have an opportunity to put forward your own ideas for your continued development and any other circumstances mitigating against your achievement of stated objectives.

Code of Conduct

This is the one part of the contract that we hope we will never have to visit. However, under the [Unfair Dismissals Act] *you are entitled to know the procedure we must follow in the event of a breach of company rules or practice.* [Wherever possible, quote from the legislation.]

Conduct deemed by management to be in breach of agreed regulations may give rise to the following disciplinary procedures:

1. Verbal warning

2. Written warning

3. Final written warning/suspension

4. Dismissal.

The following are deemed to be breaches of regulations:

- *Poor time keeping*
- *Excessive absenteeism*
- *Breaches in dress code*
- *Unexplained absence from duty*
- *Treating customers disrespectfully*
- *Insubordination*
- *Failure to co-operate with colleagues or management*
- *Incompetence or poor work performance*
- *Failure to carry our reasonable instructions*
- *Incapacity*

You will render yourself liable for immediate dismissal for any breach of regulations considered gross misconduct:

- *Theft*
- *Any act of violence*

No member of the management team will take any pleasure in having to reprimand an employee and clearly it is an unpleasant experience for all concerned. If you are in any doubts or have any questions about policy, please ask and an explanation will be forthcoming. Hopefully, none of these scenarios will ever arise but if it should, we are committed to dealing with any of these matters with sensitivity, reasonableness and in the strictest confidence.

Changes

You will be notified of any change of the above terms within 28 days. This may be done individually or by circular on the staff notice board.

Conclusion

Finally, as will be clear to you, a lot of work has gone into the creation of this contract for our staff and I hope that it will be interpreted in a manner consistent with its intentions. We need you to be clear in what is expected not only during your assessment period, but also as you progress through your employment, and likewise, I would expect you to remind us of any deficiencies in our commitments to you.

We have invested time and money in the development of our company and we cannot survive without highly motivated, well-trained staff. I expect that you will become a valuable member of our team and that is why we have invited you to join us — in turn, I trust we will be of some value to you!

If you are satisfied with the details contained in this document, please sign and return it to me and let us begin what I trust will prove to be a mutually beneficial business relationship.

I have read, understood and accept the above statement of my terms of employment.

Signed ________________________ *Date* ____________
(Employee)

Signed ________________________ *Date* ____________
(Employer)

N.B. It is a company policy to verify references. It is assumed that the information supplied by you at the time of the interview is accurate and precise; subsequently, information to the contrary may lead to the termination of this contract.

The contract as outlined here is only a sample and does not necessarily embrace all the legalities required in a legal document. It is strongly advised that you enlist the guidance of your legal people when drawing up your own contract. However, use some common sense; don't allow it to be transformed back into a lose-lose document.

In Conclusion

In the final analysis, the only true test of an organisation is the spirit of performance given by the company team. Like all teams, they are only successful when everybody is striving to achieve a common goal. The role of management is to lift staff vision to higher levels, raise performance to achieve greater growth in sales and build team effort beyond its normal limitations. The industry sets the standards, managers show by example, staff imitate their performance and customers evaluate the harmony of all the relationships. Any organisation that ignores these basic ideas breeds contempt for its own survival and destroys the greatest resource of the enterprise — its people.

Ten Points from Contracts of Employment

1. Trying to strike a balance between designing a motivating win-win document while also providing protection for both parties requires imagination — but it can be done.
2. The immediate short- and long-term motivation of your team is greatly influenced by the presence or absence of an agreed contract of employment.
3. If introduced in a positive spirit, a contract of employment can improve and maintain motivation and assist management in the achievement of business goals.
4. Before you produce a document, check you local labour laws to ensure that you are not in breach of new or upcoming employee legislation. Chances are you will also find

that you are legally obliged to supply each individual with a contract of employment — why not produce one that motivates both parties?

5. Failure to have an agreed contract of employment puts management at a disadvantage whereas a contract mutually agreed could help establish a foundation on which new relationships can be built.
6. There is little point in your company having business goals if the people who are expected to achieve them don't know what the goals are. The contract allows you to state in unambiguous terms where you wish to go and how individuals play a part.
7. The existence of a contract forces you to think through the promises you intend to make to your salespeople. Delivering on these promises not only aids the individuals' motivation; it also reinforces their belief in you and your company.
8. As staff can only be assessed on what they know their job to be, telling an individual what you expect from him or her can never be as powerful as providing an explanation in black and white.
9. In the event of a staff member having to be disciplined, the contract will become an important document. If an individual needs to be dismissed, the contract will become a crucial document.
10. Introduce contracts in the true spirit of win-win; avoid acting independently of the views and opinions of your salespeople. The real test of your management style is to give your top people a "draft document" for their input. If it truly is a win-win document, you may be pleasantly surprised how few changes and alterations they will want to make.

Chapter Seven

Motivation through Work Review and Coaching

The level of enthusiasm for carrying out performance reviews is usually low. Consequently, what is a necessary part of the manager's role is rarely fulfilled. How can salespeople be continuously motivated when managers don't take an active interest in their work or daily performance?

Work reviews can be highly rewarding growth-oriented exercises for both the manager and the salesperson. They can form the basis of salary increases, performance awards, promotion, additional training or, sometimes, dismissal. Too many managers are so involved in other tasks they have only a limited understanding or knowledge of an employee's productivity or general performance. Often, this happens because the manager has had only limited exposure to sales performance analysis or may never have received the appropriate training on this crucial function of people management.

The importance of constantly reviewing salespeople's performance can be compared to driving a car. If you don't get the car serviced regularly, it will break down. In selling terms, if salespeople's performance is not monitored against well-targeted criteria, the indifference will lead to floundering mediocrity. But what should be done between training programmes to ensure that management and staff are tackling their tasks with enthusiasm and foresight? Training with regular work reviews is the realistic answer.

The Advantages of Work Review

- It demonstrates to company personnel that performance, good and bad, does not go unrecorded.
- It ensures that outstanding performance is brought to the attention of the senior management and good people are not de-motivated by lack of acknowledgement.
- The active existence of the work review demonstrates to the non-performer that there is no place to hide.
- It highlights the strengths and weaknesses of each employee, outlines their rate of development, identifies their potential for growth, diagnoses the areas requiring special training or development and enlightens management to the pertinent function it must fulfil.
- It allows employees to know where they stand or fall; it enables them to grasp the fundamental concept that career advancement depends on their own efforts and provides the opportunity to discuss, explain and record extenuating circumstances.
- It encourages better communication between managers and subordinates and ensures that goals are mutually agreed.
- It helps to make better and more effective personnel decisions, based not on opinion but fact.
- It strengthens the business relationship between manager and salesperson, as both are "in touch" with all relevant elements of salesperson's performance.
- It disciplines managers to identify "red flag" areas earlier than normal, and enables them to take proper corrective action where necessary and to endorse or alter future plans affecting personnel.

As the review is passed up along the line, it serves as a constant reminder to managers that their role is to motivate, identify strengths, eliminate weaknesses and mould the staff into an effective sales force which has manifest impact on bottom-line profitability.

The Objectives

The work review affords the employee the opportunity to discuss operational issues and articulate concerns. The ultimate objective of motivating the sales force is to contribute to an increase in company profits. Management–staff dialogue on profits is the most motivational element of all, because company wellbeing means employee security, and responsible attitudes blossom under these circumstances.

This is just one aspect of monitoring the development of the sales force, which is otherwise only examined in the cold light of unforgiving statistics. Again, the objective is to record performance and identify ways of improving it, especially if you are convinced of the potential for growth both collectively and individually. Almost subconsciously, the manager is noting the need for training and absorbing information that will assist in making effective staffing decisions.

Then there is the other important dimension: you are the salespeople's source of quality feedback in relation to their performance, fresh targets and forthcoming changes in the company.

The objective to be accomplished is maintaining the motivational drive of the sales team through management encouragement. The exchange of information will create opportunities to stimulate fresh thinking, enabling a manager not only to express appreciation but also to show it. A simple pat on the back on a one-to-one basis can lead to motivational renewal — particularly if it is combined with some earned tangible reward.

People Involved

- *Salesperson*: The person whose performance is being reviewed.
- *Sales Manager*: The sales person's immediate manager.

- *Examiner*: The sales manager's immediate manager.
- *Referee*: Senior manager, usually the personnel manager.

It is not essential for an examiner or a referee to be involved and you may decide to short-circuit the system by keeping the interaction between yourself and the salesperson. However, in the interest of fair play, salespeople should have access to a higher authority that will act impartially in the event of a dispute. It also forces management to be objective in their appraisals of each individual.

Strategy for Carrying Out the Work Review

Work reviews are an integral part of a sales manager's job and must be undertaken efficiently and with a little imagination or even simple innovation. To get rapidly to the nub of the matter, issue a blank form of the work review to the salesperson and in isolation, both of you write down your individual assessment of the headings covered in the work review. That is half the battle, because each topic now can be the subject of intelligent discussion. Exercise complete, the salesperson signs the form, which is forwarded to the examiner, who, if satisfied, arranges for the document to go on the salesperson's file. In some cases, the sales manager may be in dispute with a salesperson's evaluation. In this case, it is the sales manager's rating that should be endorsed on the work review. Just one caveat: the salesperson may appeal the sales manager's evaluation by writing the reason for the disagreement on the form.

In the event of a dispute, the examiner may decide to interview the salesperson and sales manager separately for additional comments or information. The examiner and reviewer then agree a final work review and that version is deemed to be a valid basis for the next review. Any changes to the review should be conveyed to the relevant parties.

Performance Ratings

1. Totally Unsatisfactory
2. Unsatisfactory
3. Some Reservations
4. Satisfactory
5. Superior
6. Outstandingly superior.

The example as outlined on the following pages is part of a work review designed for a company selling to the food industry (although it is simple to personalise for any company) and the section headings were particularly appropriate for their selling tasks. The salespeople scored 1 to 6 on every discipline. The combined score from each of the sections also received a rating.

How to Score Individual Performance

The scoring system couldn't be easier. It merely requires a calculation of number of headings on which the employee is being assessed. To get the maximum possible score, just multiply the number of headings by six. To get the lowest possible score (one point per heading), just count the number of headings. Obviously, the headings will change from company to company, but for the purpose of the exercise let us assume that you also have the same 44 section headings as outlined in the previous example. The scoring would come out like this:

44 x Minimum Score (1) = 44 Total Points
44 x Maximum Score (6) = 264 Total Points

Obviously, nobody will achieve either of these extremes; however, both extremes are useful yardsticks on which to appraise performance. What the overall rating should provide is a comprehensive picture of the effort level and potential of each employee.

Section Headings					Section Summary
Unsatisfactory	Good	Superior	A. Attitudes and Personality		
☐	☐	☐	1. Customers	Does he/she display a caring attitude?	Totally Unsatisfactory ☐
☐	☐	☐	2. Colleagues	Do colleagues respect him/her?	Unsatisfactory ☐
☐	☐	☐	3. Managers	Does he/she maintain a good relationship with management?	
☐	☐	☐	4. Company	Would he/she be described as a good company person?	Some Reservations ☐
☐	☐	☐	5. Staff	Does he/she treat staff with courtesy and respect?	
☐	☐	☐	6. Job	Does he/she appear to enjoy the job?	
☐	☐	☐	7. Confidence	Is he/she confident in most situations?	
☐	☐	☐	8. Grooming	Is his/her appearance acceptable?	Fully Satisfactory ☐
☐	☐	☐	9. Development	Does he/she take time out to develop new skills?	
☐	☐	☐	10. Enthusiasm	Is he/she open-minded and positive?	
☐	☐	☐	11. Co-operation	Does he/she stimulate teamwork?	Consistently Superior ☐
☐	☐	☐	12. Creativity	Is he/she keen to acquire new ideas?	
☐	☐	☐	13. Initiative	Does he/she take initiative when required?	
☐	☐	☐	14. Motivation	Does he/she work well without supervision?	
☐	☐	☐	15. Judgement	Is he/she objective in judging others?	Outstandingly Superior ☐

Section Headings					Section Summary
Unsatisfactory	Good	Superior	**B. Job Performance**		Totally Unsatisfactory ☐
			Disciplines		Unsatisfactory ☐
☐	☐	☐	1. Presentation	Sales Aids, Briefcase, Car, etc.	Some Reservations ☐
☐	☐	☐	2. Quality	Detail, Time Management, Punctuality	Fully Satisfactory ☐
☐	☐	☐	3. Administration	New A/Cs Procedures, Reports, etc.	Consistently Superior ☐
			Shop Standards		Outstandingly Superior ☐
☐	☐	☐	4. Corporate Image		
☐	☐	☐	5. Visual Image		
☐	☐	☐	6. Housekeeping		
☐	☐	☐	7. Merchandising		
☐	☐	☐	8. Pricing and Display		
☐	☐	☐	9. Fresh Foods Development		
☐	☐	☐	10. Equipment		
☐	☐	☐	11. Staff Training		
☐	☐	☐	12. Customer Care		
☐	☐	☐	13. Security		
☐	☐	☐	14. Stock Level and Range		
☐	☐	☐	15. Financial Control		
☐	☐	☐	16. Industry Knowledge		

Section Headings				Section Summary
Unsatisfactory	Good	Superior	**C. Achievement of Sales Targets**	Totally Unsatisfactory ☐
☐	☐	☐	1. Overall Sales Achievement	Unsatisfactory ☐
☐	☐	☐	2. Individual Customers	Some Reservations ☐
☐	☐	☐	3. Central Billing Overall	Fully Satisfactory ☐
☐	☐	☐	4. Central Billing Category (A)	Consistently Superior ☐
☐	☐	☐	5. Central Billing Category (B)	Outstandingly Superior ☐
☐	☐	☐	6. Central Billing Sales	
☐	☐	☐	7. Ex-warehouse sales	
☐	☐	☐	8. Debtors Target	
☐	☐	☐	9. Direct Debits	
☐	☐	☐	10. New Stores Net Gain	
☐	☐	☐	11. Development of Existing Stores	
☐	☐	☐	12. SPAR Private Label	
☐	☐	☐	13. Promotional Activity	

Ratings

0–44	Totally Unsatisfactory
45–88	Unsatisfactory
89–132	Some Reservations
133–176	Satisfactory
177–220	Superior
221–264	Outstandingly Superior

How can this information be used to best effect?

There are numerous ways in which the information can be used:

- In the event of somebody scoring "unsatisfactory", you will need to agree a strategy to help the salesperson improve by the next work review. When the situation is revealed in black and white and the opportunity arises to discuss each heading, it is difficult to argue with the result.
- The information and results can be used by the manager to reward outstanding achievement on the basis of genuinely documented evidence, and not on the basis of favouritism. This reward may be in the form of incentives, promotion, bonus or salary increase.
- Awards can be presented to the team or to the highest overall achievers. In many cases this is the best recognition that people can be given — particularly if the awards are made public. It does not necessarily have to be an expensive prize; tankards with personal inscriptions have been known to work wonders. Holidays abroad are inspirational.
- The work review also can be used to reward salespeople for their loyalty and experience — perhaps one of the best reasons for implementing this system.

Rewarding Loyalty and Service

One difficulty companies have with long-serving salespeople is the lack of reward for long-term effort. When you have a new salesperson joining an established sales team being paid identical salary and commission, a "perceived anomaly" exists. The established sales employee feels his or her loyalty and effort have not been recognised sufficiently. This may cause resentment and jealousy towards new colleagues and a few personal motivational problems.

Salespeople must recognise that their experience is valuable, but only when it is reflected in positive results. In any profession, a person with three years' experience should, theoretically, do the job three times better than a person with no experience. How do you reward your achiever for this accumulated company knowledge, without creating incentives for those who have not put their experience to good use?

I was faced with this problem. Having introduced a number of new people to the company, some of the more experienced salespeople felt their loyalty should be rewarded in some way. I was adamant the system would only reward people with long service if their sales results and efforts reflected it. Like all sales managers, I was most anxious that people would not be paid additional money just for the pleasure of having them on the premises.

I took the five key areas of our selling operation and graded the individual performance against the following criteria for bonus payments:

1.	Totally unsatisfactory	Value Nil
2.	Unsatisfactory	Value Nil
3.	Some Reservations	Value £80
4.	Satisfactory	Value £120
5.	Superior	Value £160
6.	Outstandingly Superior	Value £220

The five key areas that each individual was evaluated against were:

a) General attitudes

b) Appearance

c) Sales performance

d) Personal skills

e) Punctuality and efficiency.

Having completed the exercise, a salesperson's review might look as follows:

WORK REVIEW — PAYMENT BONUS							
	1	**2**	**3**	**4**	**5**	**6**	**Cash Value**
Attitudes						X	£220
Overall Appearance			X				£80
Sales Performance					X		£160
Personal Skills					X		£160
Punctuality/Effectiveness			X				£80
						Total Cash Value	**£700**

Whatever cash value we arrived at was multiplied by the number of years' service and paid on top of salary for the next 12 months, when the review would occur again. In the example used here, a salesperson with seven years' experience would receive an additional £4,900 as a performance bonus.

I know of one sales manager who dispensed with the idea of a bonus for anything less than "superior" and according to her it worked extremely well. For other managers, getting people from being "totally unsatisfactory" to "some reservations" was an outstanding achievement.

The system is flexible and can be introduced in some form to any organisation. However, the person doing the review must have the guts to score people fairly. If a person has not produced the goods, their grading must reflect the lack of achievement; otherwise the company will be saddled with a costly precedent-setting system, which is not achieving its purpose. It worked well for me and the salespeople responded positively, not only to its implementation but also with a genuine effort to improve their grades. The people who had most to benefit were long established, and experience proves they can be the most difficult to motivate. There are many motivating factors in a system such as this, but it can be costly if not implemented in a proper manner. Its serious disadvantage is terminating the system when prudent company policy dictates another course of action.

One useful way of implementing the scheme is:

- Introduce the scheme at the start of your selling year (if possible);
- Explain how often the review will be conducted;
- Give full details of how the salespeople will be graded, by whom and against what criteria;
- Tell them how long the trial period of the scheme is, why it is being introduced and what it is expected to achieve;
- Ensure that the scheme has total and enthusiastic support from all in attendance — and from senior management and the finance department — before finalising its implementation.

This system worked well for me and I have no doubts that it can be applied to most companies. I introduced the system on the basis that it would apply only to people who were with us more that 12 months and up to a maximum of seven years. At the quarterly work review, if a salesperson had improved significantly over the previous quarter, there was always the flexibility to move up the grade.

Coaching Salespeople in the Field

An integral part of the work review is the occasional visit to the field to train and develop salespeople on the job. While it is true to say that you don't have to travel the world to be a geography teacher, tutoring salespeople in selling skills requires that you speak from personal experience. On the other hand, if you have only limited experience in the field, that should not prevent you from making a valuable contribution to the salesperson's education through observing standard selling disciplines and customer reaction.

Surprisingly, it is the exceptional company that actually has a policy of field coaching, and I know of countless managers who have never accompanied salespeople for the purpose of appraisal. Accompanying salespeople for the sole purpose of doing a public relations call to a customer or handling a client query is not coaching; it's poaching on their territory. Let us consider some of the benefits of coaching in the field:

- It demonstrates to salespeople that you take an active interest in their development;
- It helps managers develop relationships with the sales team in circumstances not usually available to either party;
- It gives managers valuable exposure to "where it all happens".

Salespeople can only be expected to develop if they know where they are now in relation to where they ought to be; so monitoring prevailing standards is a must. Many would agree that it is indefensible for a manager to carry out an assessment on performance if the salesperson has never been seen in action — yet it happens frequently.

Creating the Right Atmosphere for the Visit

Give salespeople ample warning of your intended visit and set the tone for a positive coaching trip. Failure to advise in advance tends to be counterproductive and creates unnecessary resentment. On the other hand, having served notice of your accompaniment, you should rightly expect to see salespeople at their best and they should be appraised accordingly.

Generally, salespeople dislike joint calls and claim it to be an artificial system of appraisal; yet the same people balk at video role-plays on the same basis. However, most of what you see — the pre-call planning, the presentation and the salesperson's ability to fact-find — will not be seriously undermined by your presence. In any event, allow salespeople the opportunity of expressing their views on joint calls and try to explain it in a way that encourages them to look forward to the visit.

Your attitude when accompanying salespeople will have considerable influence on the overall effectiveness of the exercise. Your role is only to "observe", not to teach, and to offer genuine assistance to salespeople in making adjustments, which will help them become better at what they do! Remember that the objective of field coaching is not to *discuss* sales results but rather to *identify* areas that may influence their eventual outcome.

Field Coaching Development Reports

It does not require any level of genius to design an appropriate field coaching assessment sheet and the figure on the following page is one example of how this exercise could be reported.

Before the visit

As it is unlikely in the space of one trip that you will witness the salesperson's entire performance in each of these 22 disciplines, it is sufficient to write across the report "not seen on this occasion". However, a field coaching sheet should only be completed on the basis of at least four client visits.

- Whenever possible, the salesperson's previous field coaching report should be used as a comparison of standards attained between visits. In addition to identifying obvious areas for development, ensure you are also looking for areas where he or she scores highly. This will play an important part in maintaining a positive spirit.
- Enquire how much he or she knows about the customer, the company and the potential customer's buying motives.
- A most important part of the sales visit is a clear objective; ensure that the salesperson has a definite purpose for each call.

Field Coaching Development Record

Skills Assessed — Score	0	1	2	3	4	5	6	7	8	9	10	Comments and Observations
Personal Skills												
Appearance and manner												
Attitudes to customers and problems												
Attitude to job												
Self-analysis and development												
Selling Efficiency												
Planning and administration												
Product and company knowledge												
Competitive knowledge												
Customer knowledge												
Territory planning												
Use of selling time												
Territory development												
Selling Skills												
Ability to get new business												
Initital impression												
Establishing rapport												
Fact-finding skills												
Conversation balance												
Presentation skills												
Handling customer concerns												
Closing the business												
Parting impression												
After sales service												
Post-call activity												

Avoid getting roped into active sales involvement with customers or prospects, or you will defeat the purpose of the exercise. The salesperson can rightly claim that had you not interfered, the call may have taken a different direction. It is for this reason that you should agree in advance of calls what role you intend to play at the sales interview.

During the visit

Here are some useful guidelines to observe when accompanying salespeople to customers:

- Observe the level of preparation for each sales call.
- How did the customer react to the salesperson?
- What was the level of fact-finding?
- How were customer concerns and questions handled?
- How skilful was the individual at presenting the selling proposition?
- Was the overall presentation persuasive?
- Did the salesperson achieve his or her predetermined objective?
- Was a good parting impression created?

It is not a good idea to discuss any observations from your visit until you have completed all your calls. Tutoring salespeople after each sales interview will only make them more apprehensive and they may also claim that the misdemeanour you witnessed was a one-off.

After the visits have been completed

- Give salespeople the opportunity to discuss their views on each call and enquire as to what they felt they did well.
- Enquire as to what they felt they could have done better.

- Ask how they felt about your visit. Were they intimidated by your presence? (If you have carried out your role correctly, there should not be a problem.) If there is a difficulty, it may well have to be discussed before your next field coaching trip.
- When discussing the various headings on which salespeople are being appraised, give them the opportunity to suggest how they scored themselves. With this method, the only conflicting headings will be those in which performance has been exaggerated.
- If possible, offer guidance and help on any of the areas in which salespeople have been asked to improve. Explain precisely what you expect to have been achieved by the next coaching visit.
- Write into the report all the areas on which you agree.

It is not a good idea to have any more than two negative points for salespeople to work on. Anything more will be demotivating and counter-productive. Furthermore, salespeople may become paranoid about future visits. You will see many areas for improvement — even with top class salespeople — but in the interest of motivation and personal confidence, take a mental note for the next visit and bite your tongue on this occasion. Always finish up your visit with as many positive points about the salesperson as you can. For each negative point, have at least three positives.

The field coaching report should be an integral part of the salesperson's assessment, and there is no reason why it should not be directly related to performance awards, bonus or, in some cases, commission structures. If a salesperson has a particular weakness and it is important for it to be put right, why not tie improvement into an incentive?

Finally, field coaching should be a highly positive exercise, and if it is perceived any other way, it spells danger. When they are carried out in a spirit of co-operation and goodwill, everybody benefits — the salesperson, the manager, the customer and the company.

Summary of visit

On completion of the field-coaching trip, it is essential to provide the salesperson with a summary of your visit. The salesperson should also have the opportunity to state and record his or her views on how the appraisal was carried out, but this is a matter for every individual manager. It might look as follows:

FIELD COACHING REPORT — SUMMARY OF VISIT

No. of Calls Planned ☐ Calls Seen ☐ Service Calls ☐ New Business ☐ Presentations ☐

Strong Points	**Comments**
Improvements on Last Visit	**Comments** **Score Then** **Score Now**
Areas Requiring Special Attention	**Action Agreed to be Taken**

Salesperson's Rating of Report, Visit and Coaching

- *Totally Satisfied*
- *Satisfied*
- *Partly Satisfied*
- *Not Satisfied*
- *Totally Unsatisfied*

Salesperson's Signature **Coached by**

Manager's Signature **Date Posted on Appraisal**

Rating Salespeople

There are many schools of thought on rating salespeople. Some would argue that nobody should score ten out of ten because this leaves no room for improvement. A more progressive view is that if anybody is outstanding in any aspect of their job, then they should receive a rating reflecting that level of achievement. This has a dual effect on the individual. Firstly, it is highly motivating knowing that your manager thinks you are outstandingly good at something and secondly, as any adjustment is downward, it forces the individual to maintain that standard.

Whenever you are giving a rating, allow the salesperson to express their views on your assessment and if the points are valid, agree the score to be endorsed. However, in the event of a dispute, it is your rating that should be endorsed. The salesperson can always record his or her dissatisfaction when signing the report. Salespeople will take negative ratings personally, and it is important that you should not overreact to disputes. Another manager accompanying the salesperson on the next trip can easily resolve it.

Coaching Telesales People

Many of the previously mentioned rules apply to telesales also. It is obviously more difficult to coach telesales people when usually you can only hear one side of the conversation. An essential piece of equipment is a monitoring system, which allows you to hear both voices and gauge the skills of the telesales person. This is a feature of the development of telesales people in organisations such as Yellow Pages throughout the world. Salespeople are aware their calls are being monitored but never know when.

A field sales coach would be doing well to observe 30 sales calls in four or five visits whereas the telesales coach would hear 30 to 60 sales calls in a day! With proper coaching, a telesales person should develop much quicker than their colleagues in the field.

If telesales people are to be appraised on their telephone skills, it is essential that they are aware of the skills on which they will be appraised. Prior to carrying out an assessment, ensure that the salespeople have been given a copy of the following skills and inform them that these are the areas in which they will be assessed.

Preparation and Planning

- Sales aids
- Price lists
- Brochures
- Market information
- Competitive information.

Call plan

- Who are you going to phone?
- What is the objective of the call?
- Opening statement prepared?
- Points prepared in logical order?
- Prepared for initial customer resistance?
- Concentrate for two minutes on your call.

Introduction

- Identify yourself and your company.
- Ask for your contact and check pronunciation.
- When put through: explain purpose of call.
- Ask the customer for his or her time.

Fact-finding

- Ask questions: Why, What, Which, Where, When, How, Who?

- Get the customer to talk about his or her business.
- Write down useful selling information.
- Lead the conversation and question skilfully.
- Identify customer's problems, wants and needs.
- Mentally review how you can solve customer's problems.

Discuss and Agree Customer Needs

- Summarise and agree on information gained to date.
- Ask: "How would you benefit if we could solve that problem?
- Listen and allow customer to give his or her motives for buying.
- If you need more time to consider your response, make an appointment to phone back.

Sell the Product

- Relate your product's benefits to this customer's problems.
- Back up claims with good third-party stories.
- If your solution is "unique" make sure you tell the customer.
- Give customer only relevant selling points.
- Listen for buying signals.
- Get enthusiastic about your product.
- Discuss and agree each point with the customer.
- Ask customer for comments.

Handle the Customer's Concerns

- When customer objects, listen, listen, listen.
- Don't change your tone of voice.
- Let the customer talk out his or her objections.

- Avoid pouncing back with a glib response.
- Inquire: "Apart from that (objection) is there anything else?"
- Use empathetic expressions, e.g. "I understand perfectly."

TELEPHONE SKILLS ASSESSMENT SHEET

Skills	***Poor***	***Fair***	***Good***	***V. Good***	***Excellent***
Telephone personality					
Preparation for calls					
Voice projection					
Telephone empathy					
Attitude					
Opening statements					
Projecting enthusiasm					
Professionalism					
Gaining attention					
Fact-finding					
Proposals sent					
Handling concerns					
Getting sales orders					
Handling complaints					
Effective listening					
Follow-up					
Telephone confidence					
Teamwork					
Customer care					

Salesperson ***Date*** ***Appraised by:***

Finally, top salespeople should never be rated against the prevailing team standards *unless* these standards are particularly high for the industry. Measuring individuals against mediocre averages only serves to keep standards down and sends all the wrong messages to the better salespeople. Your better salespeople should only ever be appraised against what *they* are capable of achieving. Below-par performers should be measured initially against the averages for the sales team and the immediate goal should be to lift their visions to realistic achievable levels. Managers who spend time with low producers on a regular basis will eventually reap the benefits in much improved sales results.

Ten Points from Motivation through Work Review and Coaching

1. One excellent way to keep salespeople motivated is to take an active interest in their work and sales performance — it also demonstrates that performance, good and bad, does not go unrecorded.
2. The work review also serves as a constant reminder to managers that their role is to motivate, identify strengths and mould staff into an effective sales force.
3. As you are the salespeople's only source of quality feedback on their performance, the work review ensures that the feedback you provide is based on actual performance — not on your own personal opinions.
4. The very presence of the work review ensures that rewards in the form of bonus or incentives are awarded on the basis of genuine documented evidence — not favouritism. It is also an excellent way to reward people for loyalty and service.
5. When accompanying salespeople on visits to customers, your role is to observe and help salespeople be better at what they do — not to preach and teach.
6. A most important part of coaching is not to discuss sales results but to identify strengths, weaknesses and customer reactions that may influence the eventual outcome of your sales results.
7. Avoid getting roped into active sales involvement with customers, otherwise you will defeat the purpose of the exer-

cise — the customer's office is not the place to carry out a sales training module.

8. Avoid tutoring salespeople until you have seen all their calls planned for that day. Not only will your comments make them apprehensive, but they can also claim that the misdemeanour was a one-off.

9. Try and avoid a situation where salespeople have any more than two negative selling points to work on — anything more will be de-motivating and counter-productive. For every negative point, try to have at least three positives.

10. Field coaching is a win-win for all concerned. When carried out in a spirit of goodwill, everybody benefits: the salesperson, the manager, the customer and the company.

Chapter Eight

Training: The Sales Manager's Role

Depending on the size of your company, you may be actively involved in the delivery of sales training, you may have people who are employed to do it for you or you may employ an outside agency. While you can delegate much of the pre-course research, development and design, you are the person who should ultimately decide what skills are imparted to your sales team.

Having spent the best part of two decades in the delivery of sales training, I can say with some certainty that the development of the sales team rarely receives the ongoing scrutiny or attention it deserves. As one example, I can recall a sales manager inviting me to talk to him about his annual training needs and it was clear that this was an issue that he just wanted to get "out of the way". On my second visit, he took one look at the proposal and said, "Fine, we will run with that." The development of his sales team appeared to warrant no more than a glance to get his approval.

In a subsequent conversation he told me that he had just changed his car. He called on several dealers and tested six new models and before he made the final buying decision he contacted three other people to get their "opinions". If I was his boss, I think I would want to know if this sales manager understands anything about "priorities".

DESIGNING A FORMAL TRAINING PROGRAMME

If you have never developed a formal training programme, it is probably a good idea to produce one now and use it as a template for all future sales development. I do promise that if you follow these guidelines, your programme has every chance of succeeding. This chapter will provoke thoughts on how your course might be structured, and, as so little material is available on this important subject, it will guide you through each stage of the programme design.

Before you start designing the course, there are two things you must do:

- Conduct a *training needs assessment* to ensure that training is what is actually required. Is it possible that other areas require to be tackled first, such as management attitude, new corporate policy or other operational difficulties? One thing is certain: if a manager's attitude is causing a problem with the sales team, sales training will not work.
- Recognise that training is not a cure-all. The ultimate goal of training must be to increase proficiency of performance and should only be carried out if the same results cannot be achieved more efficiently or economically by any other means.

Allow plenty of preparation time

Too many courses are run on the basis that it is a "good time" for training, or some urgent need has been identified at the management meeting. Training is more effective when it is perceived by the trainee as being part of ongoing development rather than a "fire-fighting" response to a downturn in sales.

The person you employ to do the training will benefit from a relaxed approach to the course; as attitudes are contagious, the course will not come across positively to the delegates if prepared or presented under undue pressure.

To plan the course properly, a minimum preparation period of six weeks should be allowed. A problem for course designers is that senior management may decide, in advance of the course objectives being identified, that only limited time can be allocated to the programme. As the sales manager, you should suspend judgement on these constraints until all the objectives have been considered. While it is primarily the course designer's role to decide what time is required, you need to ensure that it is commercially realistic and learner-attainable within the time period available. Nevertheless, the trend is towards shorter courses, with implications for (a) method of delivery, and (b) inclusion of fewer, but harder-hitting points. This is particularly true due to the decline of residential-type training and the global move towards distance learning.

Your sales trainer has a dual obligation:

1. To ensure that the aims of the company are addressed; and
2. To give the trainees a fair and reasonable opportunity to develop the skills to achieve them.

Ideally, before the course length is decided, the trainer should have a full and clear knowledge of what is required and embrace these needs in the training plan.

The question then arises: what can be done to reconcile a conflict between the time required to achieve desired training objectives and the need to keep the sales force "on the road"? The choice may rest between watered-down objectives, out-of-hours training, distance learning or a phased development programme.

Pre-course Briefing by Managers

Pre-course briefing is probably one of the most neglected areas of the training process. Your managers or team leaders should be encouraged to explain to each trainee the purpose of their attendance to ensure the delegates do not perceive the course as "rehabilitation". Personal experience indicates that managerial attitudes towards the training of salespeople will fall into one of the following categories:

- Those who don't know anything about the type of training their people are to receive and don't take the trouble to find out. When the people return, no questions are asked. They will be the first to say that training never achieved anything.
- Those who do know but don't consider it worth their while to explain it to their people. This apathetic attitude spreads like a cancer and quickly destroys the trainer's hard work when the delegates return to their jobs.
- Those who do know but have to wait until they are asked. They are too busy to concern themselves with such trivial matters as staff development and look on training as an interruption of the salesperson's routine.
- Those who do know about the training but communicate the course purpose in a poor manner, such as "You are booked on a course on the 27th" or even worse, "I am sending you on this course because you have some bad habits that need to be corrected." The problems this attitude creates for the trainer are endless and result in less value for time and expended money. Developing people is difficult enough without the additional handicap of management-imposed confidence problems.
- Those who do know and who take the time to ask questions about what the course involves. Their interest in the development of their staff is nearly always reflected in the positive attitudes of the delegates attending courses. The managers' genuine interest at all stages of the programme is interpreted favourably by the salespeople and the trainer. It is managers of this calibre who make learning a positive and encouraging experience.

DESIGNING AND IMPLEMENTING THE TRAINING PROGRAMME

There are many influences that will affect the success or failure of the sales training programme but none more significantly than the planning and preparation. It is imperative to have a clear and exact strategy for achieving the objectives. This strategy should involve six separate stages:

1. Compiling a list of all the behaviours and tasks the trainee will be expected to perform on completion of the course.
2. Carrying out a participant analysis to identify the present level of development, training completed to date, the learning styles and expectations of the trainees.
3. Identifying, creating and compiling the training objectives.
4. Validating the training programme.
5. Drawing up and presenting the training plan.
6. Evaluating and assessing the effectiveness of the training programme.

Defining the Objectives

Whatever the objectives, they will be influenced by many people inside and outside the organisation. How much of an impact they have on the course content will be dictated by the part they play in the overall training objectives. Pre-course research in the form of "interviews" with these people usually only involves brief discussion and can be of great educational value.

It is essential that you have insights into the needs of other departments. The question is how you find out what these are — direct or second-hand? The following is a list of people you should interview and the kind of information they can give you.

Sales Managers

Other sales managers are the people who have the most influence on the day-to-day motivation and development of the salespeople. Sales management should be asked for their views on:

- The minimum acceptable level in terms of targets, volumes and values.
- The specific areas for individual development.
- The objectives for behaviours, attitudes, skills and knowledge.
- What salespeople should be "able to do" at the end of the course.
- Who needs special training.
- What the current level of performance is by each individual.
- What training they have done in the past.
- The level of experience of the sales team.
- The manager's attitude towards training.

Where possible, you or your sales management colleagues should fill in a needs assessment for each salesperson prior to their attendance. This not only forces the manager to think of where his or her staff require development; it also encourages him or her to get "involved".

Salespeople

You cannot afford to ignore the views of your salespeople or you run the risk of missing out on an opportunity to enhance the training by relating it to the realities of the trainees' situation.

Through time constraints and many other reasons, this area is often overlooked. Usually salespeople are *told* that they are going on a training course. The interpretation put on the word "training" by salespeople can have adverse effects on pre-course trainee attitudes and you need to convert the attitude of: "They *mustn't* think a lot of me if they are sending me on a course" to one of: "They *must* think a lot of me if they are sending me on a course." Asking for their views does not commit you in any way. They will be pleased that you asked and will approach the course with a more open mind than would otherwise be the case. These people are your "customers" and should be treated accordingly.

The advantages of getting the trainees to give feedback on their requirements are endless. You can confine or direct them to specific areas by drawing up a "personal training needs assessment", leaving little room for outrageous needs. Experience indicates that trainers need to exercise caution in evaluating the importance of the individual's suggestions. It is often the needs that are not mentioned which require attention. This chart, when filled in by each delegate, can have many useful pointers for the trainer.

PERSONAL TRAINING NEEDS ASSESSMENT

What subjects would you like to see included in your future training and development? Please tick as appropriate.

Personal Development	☐	Motivational Skills	☐
Win-Win Attitudes	☐	Confidence Building	☐
Interpersonal Skills	☐	Teamwork	☐
Negotiating Skills	☐	Telephone Skills	☐
Time Management	☐	Territory Management	☐
Prospecting	☐	Sales Presentations	☐
Product Knowledge	☐	Competitive Knowledge	☐
Selling Skills	☐	Administrative Skills	☐

Include any other areas for your development not listed above. Give brief examples of why you think these additional skills are appropriate to your development.

1. ______________________________
2. ______________________________
3. ______________________________
4. ______________________________

Customer Services

Your sales course can only be enhanced by including the views of your customer services people. Try and find out:

- What complaints do you get, and why?
- What sales-inspired complaints could be eliminated by a little extra training?
- What additional information do customer services have which would be of benefit to the training programme?
- Should somebody from this division make a presentation to the salespeople?
- Should customer services people sit in on the sales course?

These people are closely aligned to the selling effort and some parts of the course may be of particular relevance to their job. You may also discover that the customer is not receiving the "outstanding service" the salespeople promise.

Salespeople may not "own" the problems arising in the customer services area but they have to live with them nevertheless. Salespeople may not be interested in steps being taken to resolve the difficulties but it is essential for them to have an appreciation of their extent and justification. There are two reasons for this:

1. They will not make false promises from a position of ignorance; and
2. Their belief in the organisation will not be undermined through lack of understanding of the practical considerations involved.

Your Customers

The target of all your efforts as a sales trainer is the customer. Phoning around or writing to selective customers to get their views on the standards of professionalism projected by your company may yield great results. Usually customers appreciate it because few people do it. You may also identify missed sales opportunities — for example, customers may be receptive to trading up or may not have been aware of the full product line. One word of caution: ensure that all questions are about your company and not a specific person. In the interests of diplomacy, tell the salespeople in advance that you are approaching customers for their views, and explain the purpose.

Analysing the Training Needs Information

The prospective sales training programme will not fail because you have omitted some of the suggestions just outlined. A combination of skills and experience will dictate how much information is required from the listed sources. However, in training terms, the time expended today in preparation and planning will pay big dividends tomorrow. Your pre-course research is important and there is no substitute for a thorough approach to a sales training programme. In summary, you need to consider:

- The specific objectives as laid down by senior management;
- The short-, medium- and long-term goals of the company;
- The prevailing and prospective market conditions;
- The credit policy and how it affects the sales effort and the company;
- The relationship of sales with other departments;
- Other candidates for some of the training sessions;
- The areas for improvement as outlined by the customer;
- The overall selling performance;
- Individual selling weaknesses;
- The areas for development as expressed by the salespeople;
- Your own "wide angle" view of what has to be done.

PRIORITISING THE TRAINING NEEDS

It is important to prioritise the needs as a preliminary to training solutions. In order to achieve this, the next logical step is to break down the overall training requirements into three separate categories: immediate training needs, short-term training needs, and long-term training needs.

It will hardly be possible or practical to encompass all your training needs into one sales training course, but once you have listed all your objectives, the immediate picture will become clear. The following is an example of how a trainer might prioritise the needs:

TRAINING NEEDS

	Immediate	*Short-term*	*Long-term*
Increase Sales	X		
Discounting		X	
Communication	X		
Sales Administration			X
Morale & Motivation	X		
Selling Weaknesses		X	
Bad Debts		X	
Salespeople Confidence	X		
Competitive Activity			X

VALIDATION

If you had designed an aircraft, you would have a test flight before ferrying passengers, and this overpowering analogy also applies to training. You may have a workmanlike programme, but the views and needs of so many people may have distorted the original objectives. To ensure this does not happen, the programme should be validated.

Purpose

- To ensure the programme addresses precisely the aims it set out to achieve.
- To check that what the trainees are "able to do" as a result of the training corresponds with the previously defined terminal objectives.
- To ensure there are no serious misjudgements or oversights in content, clarity or approach.

Method

- Pre-test by trying out the draft course material on relevant people (including some potential trainees) who will be affected by the intended outcomes of the training, i.e. the people you consulted at the preparation stage.
- Field test by presentation of the finished course prototype to a sample of the proposed trainees.
- Observe the end result carefully.
- Revise material and training methods where necessary.

Criteria

- Does the programme achieve its expressed objective for the majority (say 80 per cent) of the trainees?

USING OUTSIDE CONSULTANTS

There are many pros and cons on the issue of delegating responsibility for the training and development of staff to private outside professionals. The decision to use them will be influenced by:

- The quality of the training skills existing within the company;
- The credibility of the company-based training personnel;
- The number of people to be trained;

- The skills to be used, behaviour to be adopted, and tasks to be performed by the trainees;
- The training resources available within the company;
- The individual training needs of the prospective delegates;
- The present level of development of the people to be trained;
- Historical attitudes towards previous training.

You will notice that I have not included cost as an immediate consideration. In training terms, it should never be the deciding factor. If you decide that the best decision for your people is the most expensive, then all it will have cost you is some money. If you make the decision to take the least expensive option, and it fails, the real cost in terms of lost motivation or future attitudinal problems to training may be incalculable.

There are many good salespeople who go into sales training only to find they do not have the ability to impart their knowledge in the proper manner. There are others who have the ability to train but not the background. The success of the training programme may depend on your ability to identify the person who scores highly in both areas.

How do you guard against using inept training?

Remember that the person selling external training will not necessarily be the person delivering it. If this is the case, you have every right to insist the instructor discusses the course content and method with you face to face. After all, the success or failure of the programme is a shared responsibility between the company and the trainer. A few other issues:

- Regardless of how pristine the training company's profile may be, it is the *instructor* who should be the target of your interest.
- Ask for the trainer's client list and phone at least three of them at random: ask searching questions on how successful

their course may have been. If at all possible, talk to some of the delegates who have attended the course and in particular those who have also attended other programmes.

- Visit one of the trainer's courses in progress as an observer. Any professional trainer will welcome the opportunity to allow a prospective customer to see how successful the courses are.
- Ask to see the course materials that will be given to the delegates. This can be one of the most telling aspects of the course. Badly typed notes or boring presentation materials are bad omens and demand a cautious response.

Paying attention to these details minimises the risks involved in employing outside services. What it boils down to is that company management must select the right people for the job.

The advantages of using outside consultants

Just about every advantage inherent in using outside services has a corresponding disadvantage. What may be seen as time or cost-saving to one company may be perceived as time-consuming or costly to another. However, once you have established that the person you wish to hire has the skill and competence to achieve your objectives, these are the advantages:

- The preparation and planning that goes into a course can be considerable; getting somebody else to do it will relieve management to carry out other important tasks.
- Outside trainers are free of preconceived ideas about individual delegates, ensuring that nobody gets "unfair" or "special" treatment.
- Trainees are likely to approach training with an open mind if they have no prejudiced views on the person delivering the programme.

- Outsiders can help reinforce coaching and training already being carried out within the company. They can provide a more wide-angle view of the selling difficulties that confront the delegates — and a more creative solution to their problems.
- The company will receive bias-free post-course evaluations on the strengths and weaknesses of the selling operation.
- The trainees may be more inclined to discuss their individual weaknesses with an "uninvolved stranger".

Distance Learning

The World Wide Web has totally transformed the way people do business and it is estimated that by 2003 more than 60 per cent of all training will be delivered through the Internet. Two years ago, 95 per cent of my company's training was of the residential type and the remaining 5 per cent through the Internet. Today, it is the opposite, but I hasten to add that the switch to Internet technology was thought out and planned in advance. This is not the case with many other training companies.

Let's now look at alternative ways of training the sales force, many of which are more cost effective and in many ways, more efficient than conventional learning methods.

Multimedia-Based Learning

Many people have entrenched views about multimedia-based learning (MBL), and incorrectly compare it with the early floppy disk days of CBT. Applications were few and very expensive and by today's high tech standards, not overly exciting. Students wishing to learn through this medium were confined to simple text with few graphics and very little colour. As personal computers (PCs) became widely available in the 1980s, MBL reached a much wider audience, and today it is used by thousands of organisations around the world.

Facilities available today, on standard, inexpensive equipment, enable complex and difficult material to be presented in an interesting and exciting way on CD-ROM. They also allow greater numbers to be trained at less cost with greater control and facilitate better testing of retention and comprehension.

A given MBL course may employ a wide range of media, including text, graphics (still or animated), audio and video, to create an interactive self-paced learning environment for the user. Because of the introduction of new equipment or procedures, organisations often need to train a large number of employees quickly. MBL materials can be mass-produced and distributed quickly, and can be self-administered locally.

MBL can reduce training costs by simulating, on screen, the operation of technical equipment and systems and can be used to train personnel in understanding highly complex subject matter. The use of MBL as a training tool assists in orienting employees towards new technology and, when used correctly, is an efficient time-saving way to learn. It is also one solution to meeting training needs at short notice.

The benefits of MBL

MBL can be used to deliver training to widely dispersed sites, negating the need for the trainer or the students to attend a central training facility. Students can follow the course to suit their speed of learning and even their style of learning — including the pace of delivery. Students are in a one-to-one interaction with the computer, and so are relieved of the pressure to complete the course in the same time as their peers. If they do not understand a topic, they can repeat it; if they encounter a topic with which they are already familiar, they can quickly proceed to new material.

An MBL course can be taken in a dedicated leaning environment or at a student's own workplace. It can be used for "Just-in-Time" training, where employees need to refresh their knowledge about a topic while on the job. A trainer who uses MBL can be guaranteed that all students receive the same information, and are being tested to the same level of performance. Because of its capacity to monitor student's progress constantly and continuously, it can guide individual students through the learning path most suited to them.

A cost efficient alternative?

MBL can be (but not always) more cost effective than traditional training methods. Since MBL is usually taken at the workplace, travelling, accommodation and subsistence expenses can be either eliminated or greatly reduced. MBL normally reduces the length of training time required; costs incurred through students being away from their work are thus reduced. Students progress individually, at their own pace and, on average, training time to a given competence level is reduced when compared to conventional training.

MBL is usually a one-off expense and once an MBL course is purchased, students can repeatedly refer to the training material; this is in contrast to an instructor-led course, where after the end of the course the instruction is no longer available to the students.

Disadvantages

Of course, there are some downsides. Once the material is produced, all additional updates require a complete re-distribution. Whatever about the costs, it is not an efficient way to make changes. The larger corporates tend to have their own ideas on training and often want the material personalised for their organisation. While this can be done, whenever updates are required changes have to be made and this is costly and slow. The student is at all times interacting with a computer and opinions differ on the effectiveness of this method of learning.

WebCT

WebCT embraces many of the features of MBL and more and more e-learning companies are transferring as much of the technology as they can to the Internet. Practically all the advantages of MBL also apply to WebCT, although bandwidth considerations will, for the moment, dictate the extent of video and audio that can be embraced as part of the e-learning package. It is only a matter of time before bandwidth difficulties become a thing of the past.

Web-Based Training (WBT)

The number of course available online today is endless and appears to be growing at the speed of sound. Where this method differs from MBL and CBT is that anybody with access to a PC and the Internet can do a course in just about any subject, anywhere, anytime and at any place. There can be no doubt that the Internet has changed forever the whole concept of how people learn.

The type of technical material available on MBL and CBT transfers very neatly to the Internet, but instead of students being isolated and interacting with the PC, assistance is available — in most cases — through a "chat room". One major benefit is that these "tutors" are available on a 24-hour basis, seven days a week, to answer queries and questions. As many technical courses do not require tutors with years of experience this probably works quite well — even if the e-learning companies prefer their tutors to remain anonymous.

That is all very well for technical material but if I was a sales manager doing a soft skills course, I think I would want to know that my tutor has the required background, knowledge and experience. It was with this very concept in mind that I set up my own WBT company to deliver sales training over the Internet. I hope the reader will indulge me if I give the views of an independent person on what he saw when he looked at our version of web-based sales training. (I recognise that it is outrageous bias to present a study on my own company, but the reality is that, at the time of writing, nobody else is doing precisely what we are doing!) My purpose in quoting his views is that it shows that other highly effective training methods are available; I firmly believe that this is where the future of sales training lies — particularly where salespeople work and live in remote locations. Dr Mike Kearsley reported his conclusions in *Profes-*

sional Practice Management, a UK-based business journal and, with his kind permission, I quote him here:

> The basic approach (of WBT) is that participants conduct their training online through their own Internet connection. After registering, the participant is addressed personally and all messages and communications are transmitted through the personal e-mail system. The participant is provided with high quality, highly interactive material, which requires the submitting of exercises and comments. Each participant group will have a facilitator or tutor who is online. After submitting exercises, there is an automatic process of return but also the opportunity for the facilitator to add comments and suggest alternative approaches. The participant can contact the facilitator at any time during the program. Responses will often be in minutes.
>
> Materials for the course can be modified and changed very quickly. Case studies and examples can be taken from the participants' own work area. Areas of learning which are not relevant to the participants can be omitted, whereas areas which are particularly relevant can be included. The entire program can thus be personalised to the group. There is little limitation on the numbers of people within a group and, unlike the classroom situation, every participant can have their questions or concerns answered personally. The facilitator can monitor the areas the student is accessing and determine whether there have been periods of inactivity. The speed of modern computers and modem systems is such that the programs run quickly, almost seamlessly.
>
> Contributions from participants and from any others can be stored in a library and easily accessed. For example, a participant may have submitted their ideas with regard to the format and content of a successful proposal; they may then compare this with the contribution of all others who have ever taken the program.

Having developed this course over a period of a few years, I don't believe that Mike's summary is in any way inaccurate and based on the feedback we have had from students all over the world, the overwhelming response is that the people like this method of learning. I would go so far as to say that the post-course comments are almost identical to the comments one would expect to receive on conclusion of a classroom training course.

As you can imagine, it didn't just happen. We had to develop a system that was easy to access and use, and most important of all to produce very stimulating content and activities that would keep the students online and motivate them to complete the course. The third and crucially important feature of the course was to provide top-class tuition to ensure that students were challenged whenever submissions were not up to standard. It also helped that students were constantly aware their level of activity was being monitored. As Dr Mike Kearsley goes on to say:

> Even more importantly, the individual contribution and performance of every participant can be monitored. Participants must take part and must contribute in order to move through the program, they cannot remain passive and idle, as may be the case with classroom training. They cannot rely on other people to dominate the conversation, thus letting them off the hook. They cannot wait for others to make contributions and then simply agree with what has been proposed.
>
> Individuals are tested and evaluated at various stages throughout the program and in the case of WinWin Selling; they are required to take a final test of all the material that has been covered. This requires opinion and thought. There is no pass or fail — rather, the tutor may suggest that they review certain sections again before resubmitting the exercise. There is no reason why these final exercises could not be linked to real issues or some real research, which would be of benefit to the organisa-

tion. In short, the process can become as exciting and meaningful as the organisation wants it to be.

The great thing about web-based training is that it embraces all the advantages of MBL and CBT and, provided it is well designed, none of the downsides. A course can be updated instantaneously and even personalised for the company and the individual taking the course.

I will stick my neck out and say that this precise method of e-learning will become so popular that it will totally transform the way that people learn in the future. The global classroom has arrived and regardless of how people may feel about this method of learning, it's here to stay!

Ten Key Points from Training: The Sales Manager's Role

1. Conduct a training needs analysis to ensure that training is what is actually required. If management attitude is causing difficulties, training your salespeople will not eliminate the problem.
2. Recognise that training is not a cure-all. Training should only be carried out if the same results cannot be achieved more economically or efficiently by any other means.
3. Good sales training is an essential part of the on-going development of your sales team. It is your job to ensure that whatever training you select is the very best available.
4. When using outside consultants, it is the instructor that should be the main focus of your attention — not the instructor's company.
5. Don't allow cost to be the deciding factor. Good training is expensive but it can never be as expensive as delivering training that does not meet your requirements.

6. Nothing influences the success of training more than the planning and preparation; ensure that you follow the six recommended steps.
7. Training is more effective if it is perceived by salespeople as being part of their ongoing development rather than a fire-fighting response to a downturn in sales.
8. When sending salespeople on training courses, ensure that the reasons you provide for their attendance are positive — this ensures that they approach their training with an open mind.
9. Enlist the views of your salespeople when designing your courses; otherwise you will miss a great opportunity to enhance the training by relating it to the realities of the selling situation.
10. Look at other creative and effective ways to train your people — web-based training is just one example.

Chapter Nine

Running Stimulating Sales Meetings and Conferences

If you are capable of building salespeople's motivation, then it stands to reason you have the capacity to destroy it. The ability to inspire people will never be more crucial than at the regular sales meetings because a negative outcome from these meetings could seriously undermine your selling efforts.

There are approximately 240 selling days in a year. The sales manager's role is to maintain the highest possible standards of morale and motivation for every one of these selling days. Periodically, managers have the opportunity to sustain sales team motivation through seminars and conferences and the achievement of short-term selling goals may be decided by the flair with which the event is handled.

The ability to run stimulating meetings is a skill that can take many years to develop and frequently managers conduct these sessions for all the wrong reasons. A salesperson that has a bad sales interview may lose an order; a manager who has a negative sales meeting may cause the entire sales force to lose sales. One can only guess the impact their "frustrations" would have on customer relations.

Whenever I talk to sales managers, practically all see the motivation of the sales team as *part* of their job. I would suggest that it is *the* job, because if you cannot keep your sales people selling you will eventually have no other jobs to do!

No sales manager would consciously set out to convert what should be an auspicious occasion into a serious default. However, when I talk to salespeople about sales meetings their comments do tend to be negative:

> "I came out of the meeting more confused than when I went in! If the manager had a purpose, I must have missed it!"
>
> "I was very angry at the manner in which the manager generalised about our sales results. His comments didn't apply to me and I don't believe I should have been asked to attend."
>
> "I thought I was doing OK until the manager told me otherwise. Quite frankly, I was disappointed that he brought it up at a sales meeting. I would have preferred to hear it in private"
>
> "I hate these meetings. It seems that the people who are performing are carrying the can for those who are not!"

These are typical of the comments of salespeople, and the person who has most to gain from hearing them, but is the least likely to do so, is the sales manager. What should have been an opportunity to encourage fresh endeavour has been reduced to a morale-shattering exercise. Whether we like it or not, as managers we must accept total responsibility for the performance of the team and in particular the key issue of continuous motivation.

Meetings or Beatings?

When I ask sales managers what it is that motivates them to hold sales meetings, these are the reasons given:

- Tradition, habit or policy;
- To outline new procedures, products or policy;
- To sort out selling problems;
- To outline targets and incentives;
- To discuss sales performance to date;

- To keep salespeople focused on company objectives.

Of course, they also mention encouragement and motivation, but it is clear from the exercises that it is a long way down their list of priorities. In my capacity as a sales trainer I also have the opportunity of asking salespeople for their interpretation of sales meeting objectives. Here is what they had to say:

- To increase sales;
- To sort out selling problems;
- To put in the "boot";
- To pass on the pressure;
- To get more effort;
- To tell us what we are not doing.

It is true to say that some salespeople have a more positive response to sales meetings; regrettably they tend to be in the minority.

The Objectives of the Sales Meeting

Regardless of how difficult a prospective meeting may be, the ultimate objective must be to conclude the session with everybody highly motivated, departing in a spirit of mutual goodwill and inspired to achieve realistic goals.

It is essential that you are properly prepared for each conference or meeting and the discipline is as good for you as it is for your team. Thorough preparation presupposes you have something worthy to say; otherwise it is unlikely you will dispense quality information. In selling terms, the first impression is all-important. At sales meetings, regardless of what may have gone on before, it is the *last* impression that will have the biggest influence on your salespeople's attitude and motivation. Therefore, to fulfil your role as the great encourager, special attention must be paid to your final motivational message to the troops.

Good sales meetings allow you to get feedback from your team and to know what your people are thinking, and your skilful handling of this information allows you to perform at your managerial best.

PLANNING THE MEETING

On the basis of my own observations, the standard of effort put in by managers as preparation for a sales meeting tends to be high, while the quality of the finished product tends to be low. Too many managers are so anxious to achieve their objectives that little or no thought is given to the salespeople's agenda — they broadcast when, of course, they should be listening.

Recently I sat in at an annual sales conference with about 40 people in attendance and I list here the actual agenda as outlined at that meeting.

Annual Conference Agenda:

Corporate Plans:	Chief Executive
Debtors:	Financial Controller
New Products:	Marketing Manager
New Technology:	Systems Manager
Sales Targets:	Sales Manager

As an observer at this conference, the message from management was clear: "This is what we expect from you". Anybody who has ever presented to a group will know that the audience is saying in their own minds: "What's in it for me?"

Motivation literally means "inspiration to act". Telling the sales team what you expect from them will at least help them focus on what they are supposed to be doing, but as long as the expectation is only "one way", you will never achieve total motivation.

All motivation operates on an exchange system: "I will do this for you, if you will do this for me" and sales meetings are no different. You must answer the unasked question from your audience: "What's in it for me?" (WIIFM). Balancing the benefits to be derived from the meeting will ensure a greater level of interest, participation and enthusiasm, which is likely to be followed by more positive activity in the field.

Is a Sales Meeting Appropriate?

When burdened with a litany of difficulties such as unproductive salespeople, complaints from other departments and the usual administration problems, it is easy to fall into the trap of calling a "cure-all" meeting. Theoretically, it is the most efficient way to do it but the reality is that it may cause more problems than it resolves, as the following personal experience explains.

In my early days as a sales manager, I recall one such occasion where, in spite of my efforts, a number of salespeople ignored appeals to sort out administration problems, which held up sales and caused unnecessary aggravation in other departments. I wrote to all the salespeople and requested their presence at an extraordinary general meeting. I outlined the 15 points on the agenda and appealed for a little more care. I was pleased with my performance and felt sure that these problems would be greatly reduced.

After the meeting, one of the salespeople asked to see me and it was obvious he was agitated. He took me through each of the points that I had on the agenda and I had to concede that none of the points applied to him. He then asked, "Why did I have to travel 200 miles and lose a day's sales for a meeting that has no relevance to me?"

It was a valid point and I thought it was ironic that the person who took most notice of what I was saying was the one person to whom the meeting did not apply.

Another valuable learning experience came in the form of a casual conversation with one of the other salespeople. Don was notorious for sending in reports late and fouling up our system, and of the 22 salespeople he was the only offender.

In my naiveté, I emphasised at the meeting the importance of reports coming in on time. Don's interpretation of my mentioning it was "I thought I was the only one coming in late with my reports but it's obvious that the other 21 are doing it as well."

Without the comments from these two salespeople, I might have continued to undermine my salespeople and myself. It taught me three valuable lessons:

- Make sure that the agenda is appropriate to everybody.
- If the points only apply to a minority, find some other means of communicating this to the salespeople and if possible on a one-to-one basis.
- Never generalise negative remarks or observations. You will nearly always offend the people your remarks do not apply to, and the offender — the target of your remarks — will take refuge in the mistaken belief that he or she is only one of many.

Is a Sales Meeting Absolutely Necessary?

In my first role as a sales manager, I inherited a sales team and a tradition. Sales meetings were held every Monday morning and had been for ten years previously. Even as a young inexperienced manager, I could see serious pitfalls in such a bad commercial habit. Many people would argue that there were many positive advantages of these Monday morning meetings but, on balance, they were outweighed by the downside.

If you have regular meetings, monthly or otherwise, this is what usually happens:

- The agenda for your next "regular" meeting will be influenced by your "reactions" to day-to-day problems such as bad debts, administration problems and petty queries, resulting in the agenda becoming reactive as opposed to proactive. While these topics may be important to discuss, they will do absolutely nothing for the morale or motivation of your sales team — first thing on Monday morning.

- On a cold, wet and miserable Monday morning, salespeople may be only too delighted to debate irrelevant issues in a nice cosy training room. Twenty-two salespeople spending one extra hour in the office is equivalent to losing three working man-days in the field.
- When you have 22 salespeople all leaving the office at 10.30 on a Monday morning, there is a serious danger that they will continue to debate the meeting in the coffee shop; if you are lucky, you might only lose another three more selling man-days.

Not surprisingly, when I carried out a detailed analysis of our selling pattern, I discovered that little or no selling was taking place on Monday mornings, even though most salespeople were available from 10 o'clock onwards. I also discovered that Friday afternoon was not a productive period of the week.

The questions we have to ask ourselves are these:

- Is it a good idea to have regular sales meetings on the same day at the same time every week or every month? If you have regular meetings, you will find an agenda, whereas it makes more sense to have an agenda before you call a meeting.
- Have a look at the agenda for your last meeting. How many points should not have been included? If the points had no motivational factors, should they have been discussed?
- What impact do these meetings have on sales? Is there factual evidence that they add to the selling effort?
- Do the sales team view these sessions as a meeting of salespeople or a salespeople's meeting?

- Because these meetings are habitual, would the occasional serious message from the sales manager lose its impact or importance?

I am an enthusiastic supporter of constant quality dialogue between sales managers and their teams, but whether this communication should be reduced to regular mundane sales meetings is questionable. It is an exceptionable human being who can regularly sort out "problems" every week and still motivate people out of their skin first thing Monday morning.

If you have a motivating message for your team, that's great. Bring them in on Monday morning and motivate them for the week. On the other hand, if you have a serious agenda to be addressed, perhaps Friday afternoon would be better timing. It will not affect your selling efforts and the salespeople have three days to consider the implications of your message!

Choosing the Location

Where you choose to hold your meeting can be significant. By breaking with the traditional rendezvous, you are making a statement — "This meeting is different" — and salespeople's interest is heightened accordingly.

One of the major disadvantages of having the sales meeting on your own premises is not the interruptions that might take place during your discussions (and few people would allow them anyway), it is the queries and problems that come up before and may divert people's attention during the conference. Even the most well-planned sales conferences are not tension-free, so why handicap yourself or your salespeople by exposure to morale-damaging incidents.

Whenever I have a choice, I always arrange to meet salespeople for breakfast and then retire directly to the conference room and the atmosphere will not be infected by what happened before the meeting.

How Will You Achieve Your Objective?

Once you have decided exactly what you hope to achieve from the meeting, a good place to start is to determine the most effective way of communicating your ideas to the sales team.

So ask yourself: what special materials or equipment will be required? This will usually depend on the occasion: it can be a multimedia conference presentation with the full works or a small meeting using a flipchart. Have all your materials prepared, because there is nothing more unprofessional that a manager arriving in a fluster and shooting out instructions to an assistant: "What happened to the markers that were here yesterday?" and worse, "Will somebody see about getting an extension lead?"

The information that you dispense should be factual to be truly helpful, intelligently collated and easily assimilated. There is a further factor in the situation: Should the sales force have to do some preparation for the meeting?

Setting the Agenda

It is unwise to try to achieve too much at one sales meeting, therefore the preparation takes on added importance. The dangers of overcrowding the agenda result in audience confusion on the priorities and insufficient quality interaction leaves essential issues under-discussed. In advance of your next sales meeting, consider using the following formula. Divide your agenda into four main headings:

1. *Imperative*: Issues that must be addressed
2. *Important*: Issues not absolutely critical
3. *Ideal*: Points that would be nice to discuss
4. *Inspiring*: The essential motivating closing message.

Planning the agenda in this manner helps focus the mind on the two parts of the meeting that *must* be addressed: the imperative points and the closing inspiring message. If time is against you and the issues under "Important" and "Ideal" are not discussed, it will not seriously erode the meeting's effectiveness!

MAKING MAJOR PRESENTATIONS

As a sales manager, you not only have to take sales meetings but invariably you will also make major presentations. Standing in front of a group of people you frequently present to is one thing; presenting to a group of people you don't know is quite a different matter.

An essential part of making presentations is a thoroughly researched and fully prepared text of what you intend to say. Unlike public speaking, where even top people will not be expected to perform for as much as an hour, a sales manager addressing the troops at the annual sales conference could be "on the boards" for several days. Depending on the importance of the event, it may require you to:

- Research and compile information in considerable depth;
- Decide on the extent of the materials to be used;
- Decide on the various presentation skills to be employed;
- Ensure that the information is of relevance to *all* members of the audience.

Therefore it is important to become a supreme master in:

- Writing material for the ear;
- Controlling podium nerves;
- Planning and personalising the presentation;
- Getting maximum support from your audience;
- Making professional presentations.

Writing Material for the Ear

When writing material for the ear, bear in mind that it must:

- Gain immediate *attention*;

- Maintain audience *interest*;
- Create a *desire* to hear more;
- Project *conviction* in what is being said;
- Get *action* through audience involvement and participation.

In order to achieve these five objectives, you should start with an analysis of your audience, for which you must consider:

- What is your relationship with the audience? What is their perception of you? Is there likely to be tension, in which case what can be done or said to break it?
- Is there likely to be any intimidation in the exchange between you and the audience, and vice versa? Good communication may be difficult if this is the case.
- What is the audience's experience of this topic or idea? At what level should the message be pitched?
- What is the learning style and communication history of the audience? What methods and topics must be included to maintain their interest?

Once these questions have been answered, you will have the right information to enable you to move to the next stage — writing the subject material. Unlike writing a speech, it should not be necessary to write your talk word for word, although comprehensive notes are useful for reference purposes if complicated subject matter demands it. In the majority of cases, a list of prioritised points is all that is required, and this is where on-screen graphics or overheads can be of great assistance.

Controlling Podium Nerves

If you are nervous about presenting, you are in good company. The late Richard Burton claimed he was physically ill before every performance and in a poll of human fears, people were more afraid of speaking in public than of dying. However, it is essential that we don't confuse an incompetent speaker with a nervous one. These are the traits of an incompetent presenter:

- Poor personal appearance;
- Weak voice projection;
- Fumbling around;
- Lack of eye contact with the audience;
- Starting with an apology;
- Talking about himself/herself;
- Saying things like: "I am not very good at making presentations";
- Speaking too fast or too slowly;
- Projecting an unfriendly or cold facial expression.

On the other hand, your audience can reasonably expect you to be:

- A competent speaker;
- Knowledgeable of the subject;
- Prepared and organised.

The sales manager's inability to conform to these criteria spells danger. Long before the miracle of television, political observers wrote of Abraham Lincoln's "podium nerves". A nervous speaker may personally suffer for a couple of minutes, but with an incompetent speaker, it is the audience that suffers.

Consider these important tips on controlling nerves:

- We are all human and vulnerable. If you are trying your best, people will tend to be sympathetic.
- As most people in your audience do not see themselves as great presenters, they will be reluctant to be overly critical if you slip up here and there.

- The best antidote to fear is total organisation.
- Rehearse your introductory statement repeatedly. It may only last 30 seconds, but being able to do it without faltering will do much for your confidence.
- If you are particularly concerned about controlling nerves, produce an introductory slide or overhead. As you open the presentation, switch on the projector and you will find that people's eyes will immediately move to the screen. That will give you a moment or two to relax.
- Another good way to relax is to prepare a question consistent with your presentation that you can put to your audience for response. This early interaction can do great things to settle nerves. Make certain that the question is relevant and that it ties in with what you are doing.
- Prepare yourself for every eventuality. What if they are hostile, what if they don't wish to participate?
- Get the audience involved as quickly as possible.
- Use good eye contact with your audience; this is the best way to convey confidence and reduce personal tension.
- Smile warmly and try to convey a welcome to your audience.
- Dismiss all negative thoughts about yourself. See yourself as doing a good job.
- Use your own words, your own style and be yourself. Do whatever it is that makes you comfortable.
- When you stand up in front of a new audience, they don't know how much or how little experience you have of presenting — this works to your advantage. The only person who knows you are nervous is you.
- If you prepare well, within two minutes your fears and nerves will subside.

When I was offered my first job as a sales manager, I nearly turned it down on the basis that part of the role involved speaking to groups of 50 or 60. It is ironic that today, that is how I make my living. I still get butterflies before presentations, but now I control my nerves, they do not control me.

Planning and Personalising the Presentation

The best way to present is to ensure the presentation satisfies the six Ps; and remember, the difference between a box of coloured glass and a stained glass window is organisation.

- *Planning*: Almost in the same way that you prepare an agenda, structure your presentation, prioritise the importance rating of each subject and invest a little humour into the overall concept. If you can manage the balance between entertaining and informing, you are heading for breakthrough into the magical formula of oratorical success.
- *Pattern*: You don't have to emulate Aristotle or Plato, but a logical sequence surpasses chaotic, uncoordinated, slovenly thought processes. Order is the watchword and from your own personal PR point of view, nothing reflects more kudos than well-expressed views or opinions. You are there to enlighten and not to confuse. Build your presentation on a step-by-step basis so that it is easy to follow and consult a competent friend to advise on any inconsistencies.
- *Power*: Power is expressed through the use of your personality. Don't be ashamed to use it; break through the fear barrier and give it full rein. This means you are approaching the presentation with a positive attitude, which is the platform for the successful combination of confidence and enthusiasm.
- *Proof*: If you are making any claims, don't take chances on vague recall. Do the research, even pay someone to do it, but plant your feet on the rock of proven evidence. All other ground is sinking sand.

- *Pictures*: There are two elements here — you can paint pictures in words (parables); and you can (and virtually must) use well-selected visuals. We are a visually oriented society. We grow up surrounded by the influences of television, advertising, and various other visual stimuli. The proper use of visuals helps you to control the presentation and maintain audience attention. They force you to organise your thoughts in an orderly fashion and condense the message into a concise and more understandable story. Illustrations will copper-fasten retention.
- *Participation*: Involvement shatters the lecture atmosphere and can make the event enjoyable. Questions and answers are a "three-way street": (a) questions raised by your presentation; (b) questions you put to the audience; and (c) questions the audience put to you. Handling the latter may demand the full range of your managerial and diplomatic skills.

Getting Maximum Support from Your Audience

There are four main presentation "killers" and they are almost guaranteed to transform what might have been an excellent presentation into a circus:

- Weak or poorly thought out introduction;
- Starting with an apology;
- Giving airtime to negative people;
- Providing note and agendas — before you present.

Weak or poorly thought out introduction

If you prepare your presentation well and something goes wrong later, you have some chance to put it right. If you start badly, it is extremely difficult to recover.

Every word you utter in your opening remarks will have enormous impact on your audience and it will set the scene for a positive or negative audience reaction to the rest of your presentation.

Rehearse, rehearse and rehearse your opening comments and make them as positive as you possibly can. Starting with a strong positive series of words will not only show that you are in control of yourself but your audience will be infected by your enthusiasm. After your opening statement, your audience should be thinking: "This sounds pretty good to me!"

I recall one of the first and most important group presentations of my career. I was competing against all my professional sales training rivals and this order meant so much in terms of prestige and company revenue. I was so wound up about this meeting that I spent countless hours preparing and going over the presentation with my colleagues several times.

I arrived for my meeting expecting to meet six pleasant, friendly people, but on arrival discovered that 25 other managers were also in attendance. On my arrival, my colleague tripped over the mat and the box of slides scattered around the room. When I turned on the projector, the bulb blew. As I turned to sit down, the chair collapsed and as I fell I pulled down all the slides that had just been picked up off the floor.

The tension in that room while we waited for a replacement bulb was most unsettling. I struggled to get even the slightest spark from an audience who had already seen seven other presentations before we arrived — they were bored. The atmosphere made me more nervous than I have ever been and I only began to relax when it came to questions.

A few days later, to my surprise and my delight I was informed that we had got the contract. When the chief executive opened the programmes and introduced me to his sales managers, I listened with embarrassment as he outlined all of the things that went wrong at my presentation: the slides, the bulb, the chair, the slides again, how tense I was and how unsympathetic people were to the comedy of errors which characterised my performance.

He went on to say the reason he had given me the business was because none of the other presenters had worked as hard on the preparation as I had and I was the only one who seemed to have any understanding of what they were trying to achieve. This incident proved to me that the audience will forgive you for some things provided you eclipse it with outstanding preparation.

Starting with an apology

Recently, I was introduced to a group of business people as their speaker for the day. The chairperson's opening remarks went as follows:

> "First of all, to those of you who were here on time, I want to apologise for our late start . . ."

This is how to blow a presentation in 20 words. I use this as an example, because it *sounds* courteous, but he humiliated a number of people by apologising to "those of you who were here on time". Because the offenders were uncomfortable about his remarks, they became agitated. The ensuing interaction only added to the tension. In those circumstances, I had to call on all my skills to get the presentation back on the rails.

Giving airtime to negative people

In the majority of cases, the theme of the opening remarks from your audience will be continued by successive speakers. If somebody starts with a negative point, the chances are that the comments will be supported by speaker after speaker and any chance you have of achieving your objective disappears completely.

By selecting those you consider most likely to make positive observations, there is some chance that a positive theme may be maintained.

Providing notes and agendas — before you present

Never give people notes before your presentation unless it is essential. If you do, this is what will happen:

- While you are talking, some people will be reading, which is very distracting for presenters;
- You may be discussing page 2, but others are reading page 5;
- They will know what you are about to say — thus undermining your reason for being there.

As the presenter, you are responsible for establishing the focus atmosphere. You have a greater chance of achieving this if you keep each member of your audience focused on the same subject at the same time.

The same can also be said about conference agendas. On the basis of experience, I think it unwise to provide the audience with a timetable of events. There are two main reasons:

- You lose the flexibility to spend more or less time on topics as required;
- If a subject drags on, the audience will get bored much more quickly if they think they have another 10 minutes to talk it to death.

Similarly, when people are handed an itemised agenda, there is nearly always somebody who doesn't agree with it and that can easily change the focus of the meeting or the conference. I saw an important sales meeting disintegrate because a salesperson made an observation to his manager on the imbalance of the agenda. "I notice that your agenda is five hours long and we are only given five minutes to discuss ours". Whether it was fair comment or not is immaterial; the manager lost his head and the support of his audience simultaneously.

Making Professional Presentations

Laptops, high-tech projectors and the never-ending stream of new technology practically force us into higher levels of presentation excellence. This imposes new pressures on presenters who cannot use equipment or materials inferior in standard to audience expectation. If your audience is used to high-tech presentations, don't use a flipchart for a major presentation.

With all this technology, it should be simple to personalise presentations with company logos, photographs and people's names. If name cards are appropriate, have them professionally produced. If you can also put their logo on their name cards, rather than your own, it will be appreciated.

If you have only 30 minutes to make a presentation, it is probably a good idea to prepare your material to last about 45 minutes and plan an appropriate place to include it if you run into trouble. Similarly, decide in advance what material is least important if you have to cut it short. In making presentations, apply "Murphy's Law": anything that can go wrong, will go wrong — at the worst possible moment.

Generally speaking, audiences are extremely polite and will allow you to run the presentation your way. Unless you tell them, they will be unsure if they should ask questions as you go along or wait until you have finished.

Dealing with Difficult Delegates

What will you do if somebody insults you, loses their head when arguing their point or attacks you or your management style? It may never happen, but if it does you may regret not having prepared.

When I conducted my first selling seminar, I was most unfortunate to meet the well-balanced delegate — the man with a chip on both shoulders. Eventually, his "that's all right, but . . ." response to every positive idea got the better of me. I reacted badly to his attitude, which resulted in me having to apologise to him publicly — ironically, the session was on human relations.

I realised that if I was to make a career out of developing others, I was likely to meet many difficult people and I anticipated all of the worst things that delegates could say or do. I considered how I would deal with and respond to the most negative, bad-humoured, ill-tempered delegates.

This mental preparation was very beneficial because subsequently when difficult delegates launched a verbal attack on me, I would keep them talking until *I had cooled down*. In nearly two decades, it has only happened about three times — but it worked! Of the decisions I have made in my career, this was one of my better ones.

Tips on Making Professional Presentations

Finally, here some valuable tips to keep in mind when presenting to an audience.

1. Be a mirror of your message

Last summer, I took the family out for a picnic and parked my car beside a white van notable because it looked as if it hadn't been cleaned in a month. What intrigued me was the legend on the side of the van:

> "XYZ cleaners — specialists in retail store hygiene."

An associate told me that a salesperson called to sell him a portable overhead projector and vainly tried to describe it in a series of body movements and hand gestures. If its uniqueness was its portability why didn't he bring it with him? Remember, you are the message. As the sales manager, if you expect professionalism from your sales team, you must be professionalism personified.

2. Use the KISS method

Avoid eclipsing the main point of your message by over-communicating. The KISS method means Keep It Short and Sweet or, if you prefer, Keep It Simple, Stupid.

3. Stimulate your audience

If you were trying to turn on a member of the opposite sex, what part of their anatomy would you concentrate on? Before you continue, think about your answer for a moment or two and write it down.

Whenever I ask salespeople this question I receive some interesting responses — most of which are wrong. The correct answer is, of course, the brain! A good presentation will stimulate people by asking well-thought-out questions, showing interest in their interests and seeking their views and opinions.

4. Use the nine o'clock news method

There are few people making their living through communication who would disagree with the fundamentals of getting your message across:

- Tell them what you are going to tell them!
- Tell them!
- Tell them what you have told them!

5. Use bullet points and expand on them

One of the worst presentations I have ever witnessed came from a "key" speaker at a conference. He produced black and white overhead transparencies with paragraphs of information, which he read word for word. Before long, people started drifting away from the seminar and, not surprisingly, he was not invited back for a repeat performance.

Bullet points help people to focus on the main message and allow you to add supporting information without distracting the audience from the main issue.

6. Use a pleasant tone of voice

Try to develop a good speaking voice so that people will want to listen. Appealing articulation:

- Is pleasant in tone;

- Is natural;
- Has enthusiasm;
- Contains variety;
- Has volume and clarity.

Good presenters never doubt their ability to add value to any situation, be it through force of personality, enthusiasm or their distinct personality and style.

7. Make it persuasive

In the words of Aristotle, in order for people to change views or firmly held beliefs, they must be exposed to the three indispensable pillars of persuasion: facts, emotion and credibility.

1. *Facts*: they need a rational appeal to logically justify the new belief. The information supplied must be truthful and stand up to logical examination.
2. *Emotion*: to draw people to your cause, they must become motivated emotionally.
3. *Credibility*: they must have sincere belief in the source of the information. To persuade, you must be manifestly knowledgeable and of the highest integrity.

8. Tell it like it is

In its annual report, an airline hid the crash of an expensive aeroplane and the deaths of three people by listing the crash as the "involuntary conversion of a 747". The meaning was clear to lawyers, but not to most lay people.

Most of us would prefer to be made redundant than to be "fired", and perhaps it is less painful to "pass away" rather than die. It is quite acceptable to put a better face on a bad situation — provided everybody understands what you mean. If the answer to a request is "No", make sure that however diplomatically you say it, nobody's time is wasted with false hope when the answer was always going to be "NO".

9. Tell it with enthusiasm

The following story illustrates how an enthusiastic approach can be a recipe for success.

In the early 1960s, a cigarette was launched on the British market. It was supported by a powerful advertising campaign and no expense was spared in getting the message across to the public. The scene was of a party with happy people dancing to the music of the day — except for one forlorn figure in the corner, looking sad and depressed. Not having much luck at the party, he leaves and heads for a deserted promenade. As he stands dejectedly under a street lamp, he takes out a cigarette and lights up. A hypnotic voice says, "You're never alone with a Strand".

The advertising campaign was probably one of the most spectacular failures of all time — it hardly sold a cigarette. The subliminal message that people were receiving was, "If you have bad breath, body odour, acne and dandruff, these are the cigarettes for you!"

The tobacco company changed to another agency. They took the same cigarette, put it in a different box and gave it a new name. They advertised it using a similar party scene, but on this occasion, everybody was having fun, with happy, enthusiastic young people reaching for the new product. The company called the cigarette "Embassy" and it became the most successful cigarette in British tobacco history. Remember, it is enthusiasm that sells, not loneliness, doom and gloom.

10. Watch your body language

Audiences tend to react to visual signals over verbal signals. If you are stiff, sombre and uncomfortable, your message will also be seen in a negative light. Set aside a period of time every day to study the body language of others. At the same time, be conscious of you own body talk. When making presentations:

- Watch out for spontaneous physical reaction;
- Try to workout what signal is coming across;

- Observe gestures, posture and expression;
- Check to see if the signals are consistent with or contrary to what is being said.

It is obviously important to be able to judge how your audience is reacting to your talk. Understanding body language gives you the advantage of adjusting your presentation accordingly.

Ten Key Points from Running Stimulating Sales Meetings and Conferences

1. If you are capable of building salespeople's motivation, you are also capable of destroying it!
2. Remember that the objective of the meeting is to motivate — there can be no other reason for bringing your sales team together.
3. Set your agenda on the basis of imperative, important, ideal and inspiring.
4. Avoid ever having to start with an apology — this will totally unsettle you.
5. Remember: the first 30 seconds of your presentation are critical.
6. When seeking participation, start with positive people.
7. Use the nine o'clock news method to reinforce essential messages.
8. Remember the pillars of persuasion: facts, emotion and credibility.
9. Tune into WIIFM: "what's in it for me".
10. Give out your notes — after the presentation.

Chapter Ten

The Enemy Within: The Importance of Customer Care

The primary aim of professional selling is to create customers; the primary aim of the company should be to keep them! The importance of looking after them is underscored by the fact that there are only two ways you can increase your sales:

- Sell to more customers;
- Sell customers more.

In other chapters, we concentrated on the role of sales management in bringing about the former, but here we will look at causes of customer loss along with some positive suggestions on how to put it right!

The importance of getting new customers is something we all understand; maintaining the conditions that allow us to grow our sales through established customers is an entirely different matter. The people back at head office rarely ever match the effort expended by the sales team in getting a customer. If you can create new levels of customer-awareness throughout your organisation, the achievement of sales targets would be significantly easier.

My motivation for writing this chapter is clear. Avoidable customer loss is rarely investigated as a consequence of achieving or failing to achieve sales targets — yet it is a highly significant factor. When confronted with the knowledge that the organisation's combined shortcomings are responsible for writing off part of its annual sales, the sales manager needs to take urgent remedial action.

Reflective Activity

First of all, a few questions in relation to your present levels of customer service:

- Do you know exactly how many customers your company lost in the past 12 months?
- Do you know the circumstances in which they were lost?
- Does any one individual have the responsibility to investigate customer loss?
- Are you alerted frequently to significant shifts in a customer's buying behaviour?
- Do you have an established complaint procedure?
- Are you satisfied that the procedure is effective?
- Does *everybody* in your company see themselves as part of a sales team?
- Does your company have regular staff training in customer service?

If you answer "no" to any of these questions, you may well be passing significant business on to your competitors — business you are unlikely to ever have again!

Service is Perception

There is often a disparity between the service we claim to provide and the service received by the customer. One way to address this issue is to carry out your own research — something that few companies actually do. There are four areas of service in which a sales manager requires accurate information:

1. The level of service expected by the customer;
2. The current level of service given by the salesperson;
3. The service levels provided by the "company sales team";
4. The level of service provided by your competitors.

This research does not require a six-month sabbatical; the key information will come from being vigilant in competitive activity and asking your customers:

- What are we not doing that we should be doing?
- How can we improve our service to you?
- What additional products or services should we also offer?
- Compared against others, how would you rate our service?
- What are we doing that we should stop doing?

Many companies are successful because they make the most of their uniqueness. Visiting or phoning customers for the purpose of finding out how you can improve the efficiency of service may well make you unique in your industry. Yes, I do know that restaurants and hotels have service assessments that they ask customers to complete — but do managers actually read them, and do they follow them up?

I had been using a hotel for many years for conferences and seminars and on every occasion I would politely write on their comment forms, "Your service is great but you really need to have somebody look at your air conditioning." And sign it. In 12 years, not only have they done absolutely nothing about the air conditioning, I have never once received an acknowledgement. Ironically, it was not the air conditioning that persuaded me to look elsewhere — it was the fact that they kept asking for my opinion and then chose to ignore me!

How Customers Are Lost

Dun and Bradstreet's investigations into customer loss underline the importance of uncovering customer expectatations of service. Their enquiries revealed that 16 out of every 100 customers stop buying every year for the following reasons:

- 1 per cent die;
- 3 per cent change jobs or move away;
- 5 per cent favour friends;
- 9 per cent change for better prices;
- 82 per cent are unhappy with suppliers.

From a sales management point of view, it is disturbing to note that the greater proportion of that 82 per cent were customers who felt aggrieved that there was no after-sales contact by salespeople. While there may be little we can do about the first 18 per cent, the remainder is very much within the capability of most organisations. By working on this 82 per cent, you not only help swell company profits, you are also playing your part in securing people's jobs.

One thing we all know is that customers like to think you care about them — and maybe that is why just about every company claims to provide outstanding service. Why is it that practically all customers claim the opposite? Let's put it to the test: when was the last time you received outstanding service *consistently* from any company? (Most people are hard-pressed to identify one.) In competitive markets, customers have a choice. If we cannot give them what they are looking for, they can always get it somewhere else.

Sales managers have every good reason to be disturbed about avoidable customer loss, because salespeople tend to think "gross" rather than "net" increase when planning their annual sales targets. Let us assume that you have a customer base of 3,000 and you are losing them (as claimed by Dun and Bradstreet) at the rate of 16 per cent per year. Assuming also that you have set your sights on increasing the customer base by 10 per cent, this is the likely outcome:

- To increase your customer base from 3,000 to 3,300 is not a 10 per cent increase . . . because you will (possibly) lose 480 customers (16 per cent);
- You now need to bring in another 780 customers . . . which in real terms is an increase of 23.4 per cent.

Of the 480 customers you will lose, better customer service from all members of the company team would significantly reduce the extent of these losses — and you have a greater chance of holding on to your new ones.

Should sales managers have some say in directing policy on customer service? I am strongly of the opinion that they should — simply because he or she has most to lose or gain! What is the point in investing money in the development of the sales team to win sales contracts, if the people who are supposed to support the selling effort are not operating to the same high standards?

The Hidden Costs of Poor Service

It must be easier to hold on to an old customer than to get a new one and research indicates it is also up to five times less expensive. It is difficult to calculate the actual cost of customer loss through poor service but it probably involves:

- Cost of legal action or advice (in some cases);
- Loss of revenue through customer refusal to pay!
- Loss of management and staff time investigating the details;
- Loss of a sale or a customer;
- Loss of sales through people who heard about your company's failure;
- Cost of replacing the business that has been lost.

Add to this the frustration for the salesperson, the impact on his or her motivation and the need to increase sales by 23.4 per cent — just to maintain a steady increase in your customer base! Isn't it interesting that many people can never find time to do things properly but they can always find time to do the same job right the second time!

Reflective Activity

> When sales managers talk about competition, they usually mean the company they lose most of their orders to, yet the main competitors of the business are often found much closer to home! Here are a few questions:
>
> - Is it possible that you are a major competitor of your own business? Is your attitude and behaviour causing motivational problems and indirectly costing you sales and customers? Have you been so busy trying to make a profit that you have forgotten that your staff look to you for example, guidance and leadership?
> - Are members of your own staff paid a salary to lose customers? An individual who has lost the ability to smile at customers or the motivation to care about their custom should not be in the front line. Changing the person, their attitude or their job may be costly, but it will never be as expensive as having them turning off your customers.
> - A customer who has had one bad experience might tell countless others, who might also take their custom elsewhere. Yet little or no contact is ever made to find out why! It only requires a brief note to express disappointment at losing their business and an invitation to allow you to rectify the matter. You may not get their custom back and they may never tell you why they left, but at least you will demonstrate that you cared about losing their business.

- What about your family? Do they have unhelpful attitudinal problems towards the company you work for? Do they make a positive contribution to the business, to you, your morale and your motivation? If the points they make are valid, maybe you need to reconsider the balance between your personal and professional life. If not, perhaps it is time to bring to their attention the absolute need for their enthusiastic support.
- Do all your suppliers see you as a customer or just a location to off-load their products? Treating salespeople with disdain and fighting over "credits" does nothing to encourage support from suppliers. Key suppliers are partners in the business; developing a win-win relationship can only help to improve availability of the product, reduce aggravation over credits and swell sales and profits.
- What about the professionals you employ for guidance and support, such as marketing, finance and training? If the professionals are not making a positive contribution, ensure that they do — or get rid of them.

THE SALES TEAM?

In the years I have been involved in people development and helping companies grow their sales, I have never been able to separate sales from service. It is pointless having salespeople selling at twice the speed of sound if the after-sales service team is operating at half the speed of sense. In my view, sales and service are inextricably interlinked.

Here is a case in point and I see it all too frequently. I was asked by a chief executive to look at her company and to give an opinion on what a customer might see. To give the best visual analogy, I produced a map of Europe, placed the various divisions in different countries and asked her why I might have done this. She looked at it for a few minutes and said: "Yes, that looks like my company all right." The message was clear:

- Every division spoke a different customer language;
- Each department had its own isolated objectives to achieve;
- The exchange of inter-departmental communication was so poor that they may just as well have been living in different countries.

Let me explain each of these points further.

Every division spoke a different customer language

Salespeople are customer-driven and their communication will tend to be polite and courteous. Head office personnel, perhaps unaware that they also have a "selling" role, may offend customers with a combination of thoughtless comments:

> "No point in shouting at me — I only work here."
>
> "If your cheque does not arrive in seven days we will be forced to take legal action."
>
> "We are very busy and we will get an engineer out to you as soon as we can."
>
> "Leave a message and she will get back to you!"
>
> "Put your complaint in writing and we will deal with it as soon as we can."

It can take salespeople months to get customers, but it only take one uncaring individual three seconds to lose them.

I stood in the reception area of a company at four minutes past five one evening and listened incredulously as the chief executive's secretary reprimanded a customer over the phone for keeping her back after working hours. As I discovered subsequently, this was one in a series of similar incidents, which resulted in the customer withdrawing his business. In frustration at the continuing lack of support from this company, the customer went direct to the manufacturers in Germany. Having heard what he had to say, the manufacturers dispensed with the services of the local company. This one customer represented 40 per cent of the local company's turnover, but it didn't seem to register with this person that her dreadful behaviour had a direct bearing on some 30 people losing their jobs.

If a salesperson had answered the phone at four minutes past five, would the customer have been spoken to in a different — customer-friendly — language?

Companies cannot afford to be selective as to whom they give customer service training. It may be expensive, but it will never be as expensive as ignorance.

Each department had its own objectives to achieve

The main problem here was that the administration, technical and finance managers saw their priorities as looking after their departments, keeping overheads down and ensuring staff were doing their jobs. The customers — the people who keep us all in a job — were not even a consideration. While these departments had only peripheral contact with customers, the efficiency with which they handled queries or answered customer letters was a long way from the outstanding service promised by the sales team. Surprisingly, nobody seemed to notice that the entire company was trying to achieve separate objectives.

Very often, the sales team create serious after-sales problems themselves. In an effort to get the business, they frequently promise what people within are incapable of delivering. I recall doing video role-plays with a sales team and played them back in the presence of the service manager. When he heard the salespeople *guaranteeing* a four-hour response time to service calls he became very angry. He explained that the four-hour guarantee, apparently dreamed up by the sales team, was causing enormous aggravation with customers and service people. After some debate, it was agreed that they would no longer offer guarantees and be more realistic when quoting service response times.

If a company does not sort out the operational priorities, customers will be the victims of all the resulting confusion. Therefore, the sales manager should have it raised at board level. Strategic revision must come from the top.

Exchange of inter-departmental customer information

This company had several departments communicating with the customer, yet nobody subsequently passed on to their colleagues information that may have resulted in orders, opportunities or complaints. The reason: "We have enough to do without having to duplicate our conversations."

Surely with all the technology available to us, the easiest thing to set up is an internal customer network. Every time somebody in the company talks, writes or calls to a customer, pertinent information should be endorsed on the customer's records. In my early selling days, I worked in an organisation that actively discouraged us from communicating with one another. To get a message to a colleague, you had to go through "channels". Imagine how slowly complaints were dealt with! Not surprisingly, our customer service record was atrocious.

Everybody in the Organisation has a Selling Role

It is a simple fact of business — everybody in the company sells, from the chief executive to the part-time school leaver in the canteen. Selling, no matter how effective, will have no long-term benefits for your company if there is not high customer care awareness — enthusiastically demonstrated by salespeople and supported *throughout the organisation*.

An understandable difficulty with many indoor staff (and managers for that matter) is that they rarely extend their thinking *outside of the role they were employed to do*. For example, if you ask a staff member to tell you what their job is, don't be surprised to hear:

> "To answer the phone and take messages."
>
> "To reduce bad debts."
>
> "To keep the department running smoothly."
>
> "To deliver the goods."

Each response highlights a *total absence of customer awareness* and the reason is they may never have been told otherwise. But would staff automatically see this customer dimension if they had a change of job title? For example, converting a "Sales Assistant" to a "Customer Assistant" will obviously not change the overall job specification, but it might change the jobholder's perception of where the emphasis should be placed.

The chief executive of a major international company outlined his views on the importance of customer care in his organisation:

> "If I see one of our people sweeping the steps and I ask what he is doing and he replies: 'I am trying to create the best possible impression for our customers', I know that our message is getting through."

Is it coincidence that in his brief tenure he has turned around a long period of deficit into the most sustained profit growth in the organisation's history?

So many financial people also fail to recognise the input their department can have on sales. Although it is rarely a financial person's function to get customers, their behaviour can certainly lose them. Take this lose-lose letter from a financial institution to one of its clients:

> *Dear Account Holder,*
>
> *Your account is in arrears. Unless we hear from you within the next seven days we will be forced to take legal action. This action will incur legal costs of £300 for which you will be personally liable.*
>
> *Yours faithfully,*
>
> *P.S.* [the final insult] *If you have paid your account within the past few days, please ignore this notice.*

If this was the last in a series of reminders, the language used might be understandable. In this particular case, it was only the second letter that the customer received. Supposing this same person wrote to a customer thus:

> *Dear . . .*
>
> *You have been dealing with us for many years and I trust that we provide you with an efficient back up service!*
>
> *As the financial controller, I have noticed that you always pay our invoices promptly. I wanted to thank you and let you know that I appreciate your courtesy and your business.*
>
> *If you ever have any queries or any business issues relating to our company I do hope you will contact me personally.*
>
> *Regards*

While accounts departments spend a lot of money trying to collect bad debts, few, in my experience, will invest in a phone call or a letter to thank those who do pay on time!

Sales Enquiries — Lost Opportunities!

Why would any company spend so much money advertising their services and subsequently invest neither time nor money in capitalising on the resulting enquiries? Pick up the phone and see how easy or difficult it is to do business with your own company. You may be in for a few surprises.

Not so long ago, as preparation for a major seminar to a high-tech industry, I contacted at random ten of the companies that I knew would be attending and tried to do business. Of the ten companies phoned, seven of the people designated to take the enquiries were unavailable. I left the details with each but only *one* returned my call. Of the four I eventually spoke to:

- One sent me out a brochure for a completely different product than the one I had enquired about. In a way, this was not surprising, as the salesperson was too busy to be bothered with such trivial details as my name and company address. These unimportant contact details were delegated to the receptionist.
- One addressed the letter to "George" instead of "Pat" (these are basics!).
- Another salesperson sent the information to Pat "Wine" instead of Pat Weymes — this might be understandable, if she had not asked me to spell it!
- One salesperson spoke for seven minutes uninterrupted and never asked a single question.
- The fact-finding ranged from poor to non-existent — a crucial part of selling.
- Each of them invited *me* to get back to them.
- Not a single person followed up.

On the positive side, they were polite and friendly and each demonstrated excellent knowledge of their products. The bottom line is that all of them fell down on the fundamentals of proper fact-finding and demonstrated a serious lack of interest in getting the business. Sadly, I have carried out the same survey for many industries and frequently with similar results. It may well be that this scenario does not apply to your company and if that is the case you are fortunate indeed. In competitive markets, sales enquiries are like gold dust and it is obviously important that they are handled professionally; otherwise you are needlessly wasting company money. Consider this timely reminder from an unknown writer:

Who Am I?

> *I'm the fellow who goes into a restaurant, sits down and waits patiently while the staff do everything but take my order.*
>
> *I'm the fellow who goes into a department store and stands quietly while the sales clerks finish their little chit-chat.*
>
> *I'm the fellow who drives into a filling station and never blows his horn, but waits while the attendant finishes his comic book.*
>
> *Yes . . . you might say I'm a good guy — but do you know who else I am?*
>
> *I'm the fellow who never comes back. . . . And it amuses me to see you spending thousands of pounds in trying to get me in there . . . when I was there in the first place and all you had to do was treat me with a little courtesy.*

How an Outstanding Sales Engineer Lost a Customer

Of course, it is not only poorly trained indoor salespeople who lose sales; it can also be one of the best people you have. An acquaintance told me a story that I believe is a lesson to us all. He explained that he had invested significantly in new technology and while he was happy with his purchase he was somewhat frustrated with the frequency of service calls to get the system up and running. The engineer who was involved in the original installation and service was described as:

- Well groomed
- Well mannered
- Very courteous
- Knew his job and his products
- Technically brilliant
- Extremely helpful
- Always kept his word.

Any manager would be very proud to have an engineer described in such glowing terms. It appears that the salesperson, in his enthusiasm for getting the business, was guilty of exaggerating the ease of installation. When the customer expressed surprise at the frequency of the service calls, the engineer responded with: "You wouldn't want to believe too much of what he would tell you — I have this problem with all of his customers." Twelve months later, when this same customer wanted to upgrade, he went to a new supplier because, as he said, "I just didn't feel good about dealing with the same salesperson. I had a choice and I exercised it!" Who is right and who is wrong is hardly the issue. What matters is that a customer was lost because two people who should have been playing for the same team were not!

Sales and service tend to have different objectives. When I talk to salespeople about after-sales service, they often say:

> "If those people back in head office only realised how difficult it is to get the order in the first place, they might be a little more supportive."

When I talk to the service department, they respond with:

> "It's OK for him to talk about support. If he quoted realistic delivery dates we wouldn't be under so much pressure."

This kind of interminable bickering results in customer aggravation and an eventual loss of business.

Bad news travels fast and the business world is not a metropolis where nobody knows anybody. It's a village where people talk to each other. Everybody has indirect communication with about 200 people, so a buyer treated badly by a supplier may eventually get that message to 200 others. Someone put it in a nutshell when he said, "When I do something wrong, everybody knows about it; when I do something right nobody is around to see me doing it."

Our 24-Hour Marketing Role

Business is not only lost between nine and five; it can be lost in the evenings or at weekends. For instance; people with access to company transport should at all times display good driving manners and keep the vehicle clean and tidy. When people talk about their jobs, all too often their comments are anything but complimentary about their service, company or colleagues.

Companies invest heavily in sales teams to win business, but sloppy, uncaring staff oblivious to their 24-hour marketing role will squander these gains. The irony is that the employees involved are being paid good money while *losing* business. It is vital for management to impress on all employees the importance of maintaining the company image at all times. Every company should have proper forums where staff can communicate with each other and relate ideas back to management on how jobs, conditions and customer service can be improved.

Turning Service into Sales

Jan Carlzon, former president of Scandinavian Airlines, in his book *Moments of Truth*, claimed that in one year his staff came in contact with 10 million customers approximately five times. The contact lasted on average 15 seconds each time. He goes on to say:

> "Thus, SAS is created in the minds of our customers 50 million times a year, 15 seconds at a time. They are the moments when we must prove to our customers that SAS is the best alternative."

How long does your average contact last and how long do you have to make an impression? We should recognise the importance of responding to a changing marketplace. Attitudes are continuously changing and customer-driven companies such as SAS are showing the way forward.

Some time ago, I stayed at a number of Radisson Hotels, and as I entered the lobby I noticed that all staff were wearing badges with "Yes, I can" written on them. All communications with patrons started with "Yes I can, so how can I help you?" This may be described by some as gimmickry, but having been on the receiving end of such bubbly service, I was impressed by the positive spirit and friendliness of the staff. If we could all greet customers with the same positive mental attitude, the impact on the growth of the business would be dynamic.

Proactive customer care is an attitude that must come from a realisation that this is the way to build a relationship. Unhappily, in our profession, everything we promise in advance of the sale is subject to cynicism and suspicion, and only a series of positive experiences will convince customers that there are no strings attached to the service. There are a number of activities that the sales manager can insist on the salespeople carrying out as part of an everyday proactive customer care campaign. Here are a few suggestions:

- The buyer and the user of your product or services may be two different people. Establish and maintain contact with both parties; they are of equal importance to your company.
- Encourage your salespeople to make contact with a user and a buyer every day and, if appropriate, follow up with a brief note. For example:

> Dear Karl,
>
> Thank you for taking the time to talk to me this morning and I was pleased to hear that your new laser printer is working so efficiently.
>
> Since you took installation, we have introduced a new user manual which I think may be of interest to you . . .
>
> Kind regards.

As part of my service, I try to contact as many delegates as possible after a course. I learn much from these conversations and it is worthwhile reminding you that these people are users — not buyers. One of the most mutually beneficial relationships that I have formed has resulted from the buyer's reaction to my post-course service. He phoned to offer me a long-term training contract, and his reason was this: "The fact that you provided this valuable service without charge or expectation speaks volumes for you and your company." He concluded his remarks with a telling comment for all of us in selling: "We are not used to this level of service." I should make the point that this man is a buyer in one of the world's largest telecommunications company.

- Most salespeople would automatically thank customers for the business at the time of being given the order. Few, in my experience, write a special note to say thank you! It is not a bad idea for sales managers to do it also.

> Dear . . .
>
> This is just a brief note to thank you for the business that you passed on to me. I do appreciate it!
>
> Kind regards.

What is important about this letter is that the *only* motivation for writing was to express gratitude for the order. Including invoices and other product brochures will only dilute the spirit of the exercise. On the other hand, we can never look on losing an order as the end of the relationship; it may well signal the start of a new one. A brief "thank you" note could work wonders in future dealings:

> Dear —
>
> I was sorry to learn that we are not going to do business on this occasion. Nevertheless, I am grateful to you for your time and interest!
>
> Continued success!

Customers appreciate thoughtful gestures and friendship. There is no reason why we should not be prepared to assist the customer outside of our own product or service. Think in terms of their problems: is there any information you can also provide that would help your customer?

- If you come across information that you know will be of interest to a customer, send it attached to a compliment slip. I sent a customer a cutting from a magazine, related to a project he was working on. He phoned to thank me — the information was invaluable!
- You may also find that you can keep customers posted on competitive conditions in their industry or provide updates on purchases.
- Instead of sending the usual Christmas gift of whiskey or calendars, try and find something of particular interest to that buyer.

Remember, it is not the cost of the gift that is really important to most people — it is the thought that goes into the purchase.

Bring on the Heavyweights!

Senior management have a major customer care role, though typically they only become involved with customers when the business is all but lost, or there is some other problem. It's surprising but true: most senior executives never communicate directly with customers. The most powerful and influential people in any company are the senior executives and the power of their presence and support in the selling effort can never be overstated. How would the customer perceive it if the chief executive were to:

- Phone customers personally to thank them for their business?
- Write a personal letter expressing gratitude?

- After the product or service has been delivered, call in to ensure everything is OK?
- Carry out a PR visit to one customer per week for the purpose of listening to what they have to say?

If four senior managers made one phone call per day to a customer to thank them for the business, at the end of the year 1,000 customers might actually believe that you care!

Care Is More than Just A Few Words

Recently, I stood in the reception area of a major organisation, reading an eloquently worded mission statement, telling me how much they cared about me as a customer. I would like to have asked the author of the document: If the company were sincere in what they had written, how come all of the parking spaces outside the building were taken up by senior management and staff, forcing customers to trade excuses with the traffic warden?

In all customer-driven companies, it is essential that staff and management embrace a customer care philosophy. It is pointless for any person to draw up a set of operating procedures without the commitment to these ideas *by all staff*. If you must produce a mission statement, make sure that everybody in the company adheres to the principles or it will lessen your credibility.

The Benefits of Teamwork

Ultimately, the test of an organisation is the performance given by the company team. Like all teams, they are only successful when everybody is striving to achieve a common goal. Our role is to lift our vision to higher levels, to raise performance to higher standards and help build team effort beyond its normal limitations. Executives set the standards, managers show by example, staff imitate their performance and customers evaluate the harmony of all the relationships. A company that ignores these basic ideas breeds contempt for its own survival and destroys its greatest resource — its people.

As the sales manager, it may be difficult to unilateraly change inbred company attitudes overnight, but what you can do is:

- Make a presentation to your senior colleagues on the need for improved customer service.
- Set up customer panels and invite a cross-section of your market to offer opinions or guidance on how service levels could be improved.
- Encourage your company to set up a task force to address the important issues of customer care.
- Ensure that every member of staff is given extensive tuition on the need for teamwork and proactive customer care. Use whatever ideas you require from this book to support your message.
- Apply the positive experiences of other customer-driven companies.

Complaints — The Sales Manager's Role

I am very definitely of the opinion that sales managers should play an active role in handling complaints — if only because they have most to gain and they are likely to handle them with the consideration they deserve. Also, there are few greater satisfactions than to receive a serious complaint and transform it into a situation where the customer emerges with greater confidence in your company. Customers have a choice: they can bring their complaints directly to you or they can go straight to your competitors. Some important points to discuss with your salespeople:

- No matter how serious a complaint is, *it is what happens next that is of most importance to the customer.*

- Look on complaints as *"situations"* and not insurmountable problems — this will help you to keep focused on a solution.
- When a customer complains, regardless of how they explain themselves, remember that their motivation is to *have the complaint resolved*. The anger should be seen as secondary.

Most complaints have their roots in the fear that "all is lost". If you can calmly reassure the customer that *you will put it right*, they will become more conciliatory in their attitude. If the situation is resolved to the customer's satisfaction, you may be on the way to a better relationship than you ever had before. It is nice to hear people say, "OK, so I had a problem but in fairness they resolved it better and more quickly than I expected."

Carrying out the following exercise will prevent a drama from developing into a crisis. When you are informed of a complaint, it is essential that you or one of your people phone the customer immediately and acknowledge that you have received it. This is a key issue and what it will achieve is:

1. The customer knows that you have only just received the complaint, and will hardly expect an instant solution.
2. Your efficient response will eliminate a major cause of customer aggravation: "What the hell are they doing with my complaint?"
3. You can test the temperature and take corrective action.
4. You can express your regret for the cause of the complaint and reassure the customer that you will resolve the difficulty within a certain time scale.
5. As complaints are a great way to learn about how your salespeople sell, this information provides opportunities to make all necessary changes.

The biggest mistake that people make when handling serious complaints is to fuel the fire of annoyance by not getting back to the customer quickly enough. Applying this principle will not eliminate serious complaints, but it will make them easier to handle.

And a final reminder:

> *Outstanding service never happens by accident.*
> *It is always the result of outstanding teamwork*
> *by motivated people supported by enthusiastic*
> *management selling goods and services*
> *to customers who know you care.*

Ten Key Points on the Enemy Within

1. Most of the business we lose could be avoided.
2. Everybody in the company sells — get them on your side!
3. Enlist the support of senior management colleagues to improve customer care.
4. Service is more than just a few words; it has to be followed by action.
5. Give a little extra — go above and beyond the sale!
6. Changing a job title may help staff change their perceptions on where to place the emphasis.
7. Look after your buyers' customers.
8. A complaint is never as important as *what happens next*.
9. Complaints are an opportunity to increase customer goodwill.
10. By making customers' problems your problems, you become more than just another supplier — you become a friend.

Chapter Eleven

Setting and Achieving Sales Targets

You are unlikely to lift the performance of your sales team unless you also lift their vision of what their job is all about. If underachievers enter into a new selling campaign, replicating all the sins of the past, performance cannot and will not improve. It stands to reason that if you always do what you have always done, you will only get what you have always got!

There are two main ways in which sales managers can bring about a change in salespeople's performance and ensure the achievement of sales targets:

- Help them identify, through simple analysis, which of their sales activities require a new approach. This allows salespeople to separate selling strengths from weaknesses.
- Help salespeople to understand the activities they need to carry out in order to set and achieve sales targets.

There really isn't a downside to exploring new ways of helping salespeople. It boost a salesperson's confidence when you begin by acknowledging their strengths, then it directly benefits them when you are able to rectify a major cause of their sales failure. The salesperson earns more money, you get your rewards and your company increases its sales.

Reflective Activity

First of all, a few questions about how your people sell. If you were to put these questions to your sales team, would they be in a position to provide the answers?

- How many telephone calls do they need to make to get a fact-finding interview?
- How many fact-finding interviews result in a proposal/quotation?
- How many proposals/quotations result in a sale?

Chances are that neither you nor your salespeople can answer these questions. Yet this information is critical to their development as sales achievers — and yours as a successful sales manager. How can you help a salesperson eliminate a serious weakness if you don't know what or where that weakness is?

A deficiency in one selling area can create a domino effect throughout all other selling activities. A weakness in getting telephone appointments means fact-finding visits are reduced; fewer proposals are created, resulting in even fewer sales. You must assist salespeople to distinguish the difference between efficiency and effectiveness in selling. Efficiency is doing the right job whereas effectiveness is doing the job right. For example, a salesperson who is efficient at making calls but whose efforts do not result in quality appointments can hardly be described as effective. The solution is not a generic sales course but a couple of hours in the presence of a professional sales trainer with a very specific agenda — qualifying prospects.

On the other hand, a salesperson may have a very high call rate, but his or her failure to carry out proper fact-finding will always result in poor conversion rates. It is then incorrectly assumed that the salesperson must have a problem in "closing" and special training is provided. As "closing" wasn't the salesperson's difficulty in the first place, poorly focused training only amplifies the problem. One can only imagine what this shabby diagnosis will do for the salesperson's confidence.

COMMON CAUSES OF SALES FAILURE

It has been my experience that most sales managers cannot correctly identify a salesperson's skill deficiency. This is not surprising when you consider that it is the exceptional manager who goes out on calls for the purpose of identifying and eliminating selling weaknesses. But where are the normal weaknesses and how do you identify them? Let us look at the most common causes of sales failure and take a mental note of the points that apply to your sales team.

- Not taking enough time out to learn about their own and their competitor's products. I find it amazing that so many professional salespeople cannot list the Unique Selling Points of their products or their company. If salespeople cannot make the most of their uniqueness, how can they hope to have a competitive edge over rivals?
- If there is one profession where creative thinking is an advantage, it is that of the salesperson. The key to successful selling is not only a capacity for hard work but also the ability to work smart. Usually the effort expended in sending aimless mail-shots is not worth the time invested, so why bother? The smarter salespeople will probably write three personal letters a day to prospective customers and then follow them up with a phone call the following week.
- Few salespeople write down key points of what they want to say on the phone. Buyers are busy people; the longer salespeople waffle on about their products, the less chance they have of getting to meet the buyer. It is the exceptional salespeople who can discipline themselves not to sell on the phone when the objective was only to get an appointment.
- Some salespeople are too lazy to find out basic details about the client company before they make that all-important first

call. A phone call, a visit to the web site or a brief look at the company's listing in the Yellow Pages may provide valuable information. Being able to use this knowledge in the fact-finding interview can be the difference between succeeding and failing in building relationships.

- Going out into the field looking for sales as opposed to looking for customers. As discussed in an earlier chapter, if you depend on repeat business, this is not the attitude that salespeople should display. Buyers are screaming at us: *if your only motivation is to get a sale — don't bother calling!*
- Salespeople need to make a decision on whether they are in the one-, two- or multiple-call close business. If you sell products that require the customer to compare and consider, your people are only wasting valuable selling opportunities by trying to force a decision when the buyer is not in a position to make one — yet!
- Unclear call objective. Again, it appears to be the exceptional salesperson that can carry out a brief icebreaker and explain in very clear terms what he or she intends to do on the call. Failure to use simple phrases such as: *the purpose of my call* usually results in losing control of what should have been a fact-finding interview. The salesperson falls into defending their product and answering objections — a dialogue that has "no sale" written all over it.
- Failure to understand that this is only a fact-finding call and the sole purpose is to get information. This is the critical stage of the interview and where most sales are lost by salespeople who cannot resist the temptation to sell! Fact-finding and selling are two separate disciplines — they do not happen together.
- When salespeople get to the proposal stage they have already done 90 per cent of the work, but the remainder is the 10 per cent they get paid for. Why is it that so many salespeople blow their chances with a standard "off the shelf"

quotation that bears little resemblance to the fact-finding discussion? The proposal document should clearly state: *I understand your problem; here is our personalised solution.* As a sales manager I would want to see every proposal until I am satisfied that each salesperson is capable of producing something that has a real chance of getting the business.

- Finally, not taking time out to upgrade their skills. How can a salesperson remain sharp and competitive if they fail to keep in touch with an ever-changing market place? Macys in New York claim that over 50 per cent of the products in their store were not even in existence five years ago. Buyers too are exposed to higher levels of professional selling than ever before. What chance would you give to the salesperson who thinks that a few days' sales training is sufficient in a profession that many of us have spent half a lifetime trying to understand?

You will have noted that not once has a salesperson's inability to "close the sale" been listed as a major cause of sales failure. This is a fascinating contradiction, because the sales training demanded by practically all sales managers is that their salespeople be better at "closing".

Reflective Activity

Based on what you have just read:

- How many of the previous ten points apply to your team of salespeople?
- How much does the way your people sell affect your total sales achievement?
- How much better would they be at their job if proper coaching was provided?
- Whose job is it to provide coaching and to ensure that salespeople sell correctly?

When a salesperson is making calls and not getting sales it may well be that his or her failure may be down to something very simple. However, unless the deficiency is corrected, failure is sure to continue. So, when you are sending people out, ensure that the way they sell is not a major cause of your company losing sales. This is the first and most important principle in helping salespeople to achieve sales targets!

IDENTIFYING SELLING STRENGTHS AND WEAKNESSES

There are alternatives to going into the field to monitor your salespeople's activities and one excellent way is to have your salespeople complete periodic activity analysis sheets. Good territory management and better time use will at best only increase their efficiency and will not always be reflected in extra sales. On the other hand, when their activities are centred on identified effective selling tasks, selling productivity is assured.

Have a look at these Day Planners, Week Planners and Activity Analysis forms reproduced on the following pages. They can be easily reproduced on 3" x 5" cards. The feedback from salespeople who use them is consistent with my original objective when designing them, which was to:

- Encourage a disciplined approach to selling;
- Discipline salespeople to plan each day;
- Stress the need for daily sales targets;
- Provide a basis for "actual" activity analysis;
- Identify selling areas requiring special attention;
- Establish new disciplines in sales-oriented self-development.

If you want to analyse your salespeople's selling productivity, have your people complete the cards every day for one month and you will have substantial information for an individual productivity analysis.

DAY PLANNER (FRONT)

Sales Day Planner	***Name:***		***Day:***	
Contact's Name	**Phone No.**	**Comments**	**Today's Targets**	**No.**
			Telephone Appt.	
			Customer Service	
			Canvass Calls	
			Sales Calls	
			Presentations	
			Sales Orders	
			Mail Shots	
			New Leads	
			Quotations	

DAY PLANNER (BACK)

Time	Appointments and Meetings
08.30	
09.00	
09.30	
10.00	
10.30	
11.00	
11.30	
12.00	
12.30	
Lunch	
02.00	
02.30	
03.00	
03.30	
04.00	
04.30	
05.00	
05.30	
Eve	

WEEK PLANNER (FRONT)

Weekly Sales Planner				***Week Ending:***	
Time	**Monday**	**Tuesday**	**Wednesday**	**Thursday**	**Friday**
a.m.					
p.m.					

WEEK PLANNER (BACK)

Selling Activity	**Achieved Last Week**	**Target for This Week**	**Imperative Tasks**	**Important, Not Imperative**
Telephone Appts.				
Customer Service				
Canvass Calls				
Sales Calls				
Presentations				
Sales Orders			**Notes/Reminders/Follow-up**	
Mail Shots				
New Leads				
Quotations				

ACTIVITY ANALYSIS CARD (FRONT)

Activity Analysis	***For Period:***	
Telephone Activity	**Field Selling Activity**	**Time Management**
Number of calls made	Total calls	Time travelling
Customer service type	Canvassing	Waiting on buyers
Total calls for appts	Customer service	Administration
Number appts. gained	Presentations	Sales meetings
Success rate of appts. %	Sales orders	Miscellaneous
	Success rate on calls %	Total miles
Mail Shots	**Quotations**	**Productive Selling**
Sent out	Delivered	Hours worked
Response	Sold	Non-productive hours
Success rate %	Success rate %	% time lost

ACTIVITY ANALYSIS CARD (BACK)

Selling Activity Success Rates	
Telephone calls to appts.	%
Calls to sales orders	%
Presentations to sales	%
Mail shots	%
Quotations	%
Productive selling time	%
Miles per sale	%
Areas for Special Attention	
Making appointments by telephone	☐
Customer service calls	☐
Canvassing for new business	☐
Sales calls	☐
Presentations	☐
Sales orders	☐
Mail shots	☐
New leads	☐
Quotations	☐
Time in the field	☐
Mileage	☐

Need for Honest Analysis

Many salespeople are bad administrators and may look on these cards as extra paperwork, particularly when it is obvious that they do not replace a diary. However, my experience suggests that once salespeople get into the habit of using them, they find it difficult to operate without them. While most sales organisations have their own call and order analysis sheets, I have often found that they are ineffective. Salespeople may enter what they believe the manager expects to read — which often bears little resemblance to what actually happened during the selling day. Proper use of these cards will give accurate information on the following:

- Success rate on telephone calls to appointments made;
- Success rate on visits made to sales gained;
- Number of presentations to gain an order;
- Success rate on quotations delivered to orders received;
- Total miles travelled to receive an order;
- Total time lost during the analysis period;
- Areas requiring special attention by the salesperson.

I give you my absolute assurance that if you can persuade your salespeople to carry out this analysis for just one month, you will be amazed at the information it will provide — and so will they!

Using the Sales Planners

Producing the cards is straightforward: copy them or, if you prefer, produce your own. The headings under "Today's Targets" can be tailored to suit your own organisation. At the end of each week, the information should be transferred to the "Weekly Sales Planner". After a period of four weeks, transfer the information to the "Activity Analysis" cards. It is most useful (but certainly not essential) if a record is kept of business mileage over the corresponding period.

Carrying out such analysis periodically will give your selling productivity a boost, provided you ensure that they put the information to good use. Even the most successful salespeople should not consider themselves above the exercise: it is often the high fliers who have most to gain.

YOUR POTENTIAL FOR EXTRA SALES

I truly believe that if you picked ten salespeople at random and gave them sales targets equivalent to one per cent of the sales potential of that particular territory — they would still only come in with one per cent. The reason is that salespeople usually make the mistake of looking at their territory in terms of how they will achieve a specific sales target. In my opinion, this is the total opposite of what should happen. They should know that the territory is capable of yielding significantly more than they are being asked to produce.

One thing you can do prior to setting team targets is to have a brainstorming session on something totally unrelated to sales achievement. In the true spirit of creative thinking, salespeople are only allowed to come up with positive ideas. It was Edison who said that the brain could be trained in the same way as we train other parts of the body. If you can get your people to operate in a stimulating environment for a period of time, you will certainly have a greater chance of a positive outcome if a discussion on targets follows shortly thereafter. It may also alter the salespeople's mindset from *how I will not* to *how I will!*

Negative Influences

One of the most educational experiences in my career was in my second job as a salesperson. As I had two weeks to wait for my induction course, my sales manager agreed to let me out in the field to get acquainted with my new territory. I was given no sales targets or training. In those two weeks, I worked entirely on my own and opened up 17 new accounts without any difficulty whatsoever.

When I attended the induction, my sales colleagues and managers made such a big deal about my achievement that I slowly began to believe that my first two weeks must have been a "freak" performance. When I returned to my territory, I discovered that everything they had said about the job was absolutely correct. I started to see all the things that were wrong with the job, the lack of support from head office, rude customers, moody managers and a whole series of other circumstances that prevented me from selling efficiently.

Up to the time I finished in that company, I never even came close to replicating the performance of those first two weeks. Being young and inexperienced, I was unaware of the very negative effect of other people's opinions on my self-belief. This personal experience has alerted me to the importance of keeping new people away from the many negative influences to which they may be exposed. I have also developed the habit of not giving salespeople targets until after they have demonstrated what they can do without imposing a "ceiling". Next time you are bringing in a new product, send your people out and see what they can do.

Setting all the "Agendas"

When you sit down to plan your annual sales campaign, this is also the time to set all of your year's objectives. The following will influence your planning:

- Your company's objectives:
    - Long- and short-term goals
    - Sales targets
    - New business development
    - Other departmental objectives
- Your customers' objectives:

    - How often they want your salespeople to call
    - What they want your people to do when they get there
    - How long your salespeople should spend on a visit
- Your salespeople's personal objectives:
    - Earnings
    - Promotion
    - Job satisfaction.

Your sales team is doomed to failure, however, if you do not include all of these objectives in your plan. It is important to recognise the role these objectives can play in keeping your salespeople focused and motivated to sell throughout the year.

Setting the Targets

It is a most unusual sales team where everybody is on target at the end of the selling year. More often than not, some are struggling to make quota. One reason why salespeople find themselves under pressure in the last quarter of the year is because they have fallen so far behind that catching up has become a monumental task. Listed here are many of the contributing factors:

- Failure to set targets early enough. Management is often responsible, giving the sales team their budgets when the New Year is already several weeks old!
- Wasting positive selling time convincing themselves that targets are unachievable rather than getting down to serious planning.
- Robbing Peter to pay Paul. In an effort to achieve year-end results, normal prospecting is put on hold and all efforts go into "closing" all outstanding proposals. This frequently results in salespeople having no "live" proposals to work with in the new selling year. It is further compounded by the fact

that, as normal selling activity was suspended, the supply of appointments, fact-finders and proposals is much too low to meet the first month's targets.

- Failure to set targets properly and monitor progress. Salespeople rarely concern themselves about targets until it is obvious that they have fallen behind. What started out as a target of one sale per day becomes 1. 5, then 2. 0, then 2. 5, and this is undoubtedly a huge contributor to sales failure.

Helping Salespeople Set Activity Targets

I am very strongly of the opinion that every salesperson is personally responsible for the achievement of their targets. The onus, therefore, is also on them to set up a system that alerts them to any surprises. After all, they are the people who have most to gain from the implementation of any system that helps keep them on target. The reality is they may not know how to develop a system. To create one will require a combined effort from you and your salespeople. It may be tedious but it is worth every moment invested.

Apply Murphy's Law

As we know, anything that can go wrong will go wrong at the worst possible time. Plan your year on the basis of some things not going according to plan. A big order is cancelled, half the sales force get flu and you lose your top customer. Taking all these factors into consideration, by how much do you think you should increase your targets to ensure that you achieve at least 100 per cent of budgeted sales?

Monthly Targets — Planning for Failure

A cardinal mistake by salespeople is to take their annual target (say 1,200,000) and divide it by twelve to work out the monthly quota (100,000) — this will inevitably cause problems. What is not taken into account is:

- Some months have five weeks while others have four;

- Public holidays apply to some months and not to others;
- Annual leave impacts monthly sales, but adjustments are rarely made;
- Scheduled days for training or sales meetings are not usually included
- Seasonality affects certain products and markets in different ways.

Because we know that each month is not equitable, it is wise to get salespeople to build the inequity into their annual planning. So instead of the year being broken into 12 equal targets, as in Example A below, it more closely resembles Example B. Note also that Example B includes a 5 per cent safety net.

Example A		**Example B**	
January	100,000	January	111,500
February	100,000	February	100,500
March	100,000	March	130,000
April	100,000	April	130,000
May	100,000	May	130,000
June	100,000	June	95,000
July	100,000	July	85,000
August	100,000	August	40,000
September	100,000	September	110,000
October	100.000	October	120,000
November	100,000	November	110,000
December	100,000	December	80,000

Calculate the actual number of days available to sell

The number of available selling days is obviously important because they dictate daily targets. Use the following chart as a guide and have your salespeople work out the number of days they can logically expect to be able to sell. If regular time is spent in the office, the corresponding number of days needs to listed. To Deduct from 365 Days:

• Weekends	120 days
• Annual holidays	25 days
• Public holidays	8 days
• Sales meetings	12 half-days or 6 days
• Illness/personal business	5 days
• Days left to sell!	201 days

Now we know there are only 201 selling days. Here is an interesting activity: Take any salesperson's sales results at random, divide his or her target by 201 and then multiply that figure by the number of working days to date. Taking seasonal and other factors into account, if that salesperson's performance is not at or above that figure — unless they have some great prospects — they will probably struggle to achieve target.

Number of Calls to Fact Finders

Ask your salespeople to take out their diaries, sales reports or any other pertinent information they may have available. This is where the activity analysis as mentioned earlier in this chapter could play a huge supporting role.

The longer the period of appraisal, the more secure the information. Ideally, if your people have accurate statistics going back over 12 months, the data is of greater value than if appraising a performance over a shorter period — but if that is all you have to work on, then so be it!

Whatever period is selected to appraise your team's performance, they must use exactly the same period for the rest of the calculations on fact finders and proposals.

- Count up the number of visits made to buyers.
- Extract the number of fact-finders completed.

- Divide number of fact-finders by the number of calls.

This will provide you with the salesperson's hit rate on fact-finders. You now know that he or she needs to make "X" number of calls to get one fact-finder.

Number of Fact Finders to a Proposal

Apart from the fact that this information is invaluable to achieving targets, it also highlights the need for urgent action if the figures indicate a serious weakness in any element of the salesperson's performance! This information will not only assist in improving hit rates; it also indicates the quality of the calls.

- How many fact-finders completed?
- How many resulted in a proposal/quotation?
- Divide fact-finders into number of proposals.

This will give you the hit rate. You now know that the salesperson needs to complete "Y" fact-finders to get one proposal.

Number of Proposals to Sales

The only information required in this crucial part of the exercise is the number of sales gained from proposals. Any outstanding proposals should not be included. Using the exact same period as you used to uncover your fact-finding rate:

- How many proposals were sent out/delivered?
- How many resulted in a sale?
- Divide number of successes into number of proposals.

This will give you a hit rate. This salesperson needs to submit "Z" proposals to get one sale.

Information Now Available

If you can encourage your salespeople to accumulate this valuable data, they should have little difficulty in not only achieving targets but exceeding them. Now what we know is this:

- How much we need to inflate the sales target to account for Murphy's Law;
- How to target individual months;
- The average sale (revenue into number of sales);
- Number of calls to a fact-finder;
- Number of fact-finders to a proposal;
- Number of proposals to a sale.

Let us see how this information can assist the salesperson in setting the annual target.

Setting your Sales Target

By following these simple steps, there is absolutely no reason why your salespeople cannot predict with some precision what should happen throughout the coming selling year! They should see this as their own personal sales management system.

Revenue Targets

Annual Sales Target	1,200,000
Safety Net	50,000
Target to be achieved	1,250,000

Annual Activity Targets

Number of days to sell	201
Sales required to reach target	250
Sales required per day	1.24
Value of average sale	5,000

Daily Activity Targets

Sales calls to be completed	8
Fact-finders to be completed	6
Proposals to be submitted	5
Sell 2 in 5 proposals	@ 5,000 per sale
250 sales @ 5,000 per sale	= 1,250,000

Measuring and Monitoring

It is important that the system be monitored from day one; you and your salespeople have everything to gain and absolutely nothing to lose. If they go astray, the monitoring will clearly indicate that corrective action is required. It allows salespeople to spread effort over the selling year. It also prevents serious pressures in the last few weeks — which directly affect motivation and attitude for the next selling campaign!

FINALLY, A FEW WORDS OF COMFORT!

Any sales manager who can get the sales team to apply these fundamentals to sales targeting has an excellent chance of achieving budgeted sales consistently. By applying these principles, you will also improve the quality of the prospects that your salespeople visit and individual performances. It will significantly improve fact-finding skills and increase hit rates on proposals. The combination of these positive activities will dramatically increase sales, company profits and your salespeople's earnings.

TEN KEY POINTS ON SETTING AND ACHIEVING SALES TARGETS

1. Help your people decide which sales activities need a new approach.
2. The law of averages also applies to selling — increased calls means increased sales.

3. Forget about "closing sales" — help salespeople concentrate on "opening".
4. Many annual sales campaigns founder before the year even starts because salespeople lack the conviction that their targets can be achieved.
5. Get salespeople to keep a constant daily record of calls, fact-finders, proposals and sales.
6. When effective selling tasks are identified, selling productivity is assured.
7. Beware the "domino effect": one activity weakness can create others.
8. Get salespeople thinking positively before you discuss sales targets.
9. Beware of negative conditioning with new salespeople.
10. Remember: if you always do what you have always done, you will only get what you have always got!

Bibliography

Carlzon, Jan (1989), *Moments of Truth*, Cambridge, MA: Ballinger Publishing.

Carnegie, Dale (1981), *How to Win Friends and Influence People*, New York: Pocket Books, Simon and Schuster.

Coue, Emile (1980), *Self-Mastery Through Conscious Autosuggestion*, 13th Impression, New York: Alan Unwin Inc.

Covey, Stephen (1989), *The 7 Habits of Highly Effective People*, New York: Simon and Schuster.

Fenton, John (1999), *How to Double Your Profits Within the Year*, London: Management Books 2000.

Iacocca, Lee (1987), *Iacocca*, New York: Bantam Books.

Maltz, Maxwell (1980), Psycho-Cybernetics: A New Technique for Using Your Subconscious Power, Wellingborough, Northants: Thorsons Publishers Ltd.

Mercer, David (1988), *The Sales Professional: Strategies for Managing the High Level Sale*, London: Kogan Page Ltd.

Rodgers, Buck, *The IBM Way*, New York: Simon and Schuster.

Index